THE
MYSTERY
OF
CONSCIOUSNESS

A PRESCRIPTION FOR
HUMAN SURVIVAL

OTHER WORKS BY RUTH NANDA ANSHEN

Morals Equals Manners

Anatomy of Evil

Biography of an Idea

Reality of the Devil

SERIES FOUNDER

ANSHEN TRANSDISCIPLINARY LECTURESHIPS

IN ART, SCIENCE AND THE PHILOSOPHY OF CULTURE

CONVERGENCE

CREDO PERSPECTIVES

PERSPECTIVES IN HUMANISM

RELIGIOUS PERSPECTIVES

SCIENCE OF CULTURE

TREE OF LIFE

WORLD PERSPECTIVES

THE
MYSTERY
OF
CONSCIOUSNESS

A PRESCRIPTION FOR
HUMAN SURVIVAL

by Ruth Nanda Anshen

MOYER BELL

WAKEFIELD, RHODE ISLAND & LONDON

Published by Moyer Bell

First Edition

**LIBRARY OF CONGRESS
CATALOGING IN PUBLICATION DATA**

Anshen, Ruth Nanda.
   The mystery of consciousness / by
Ruth Nanda Anshen. — 1st ed.
     p.   cm.
   Includes index.
   1. Consciousness. 2. Self (Philosophy) I. Title.
B808.9.A57   1994   93-46334
126—dc20   CIP

1-55921-116-4

Printed in the United States of America
Distributed in North America by Publishers Group West, P.O. Box 8843, Emeryville, CA 94662 800-788-3123 (in California 510-658-3453) and in Europe by Gazelle Book Services Ltd., Falcon House, Queen Square, Lancaster LA1 1RN England 524-68765.

Dedication
To

Paul Oscar Kristeller who has rescued the human Mind through his supernal erudition, his preservation of the classical Greek, Latin, Mediaeval and Renaissance Philosophy, the seminal sources of our Western culture, Tradition, and who also nourished the Mind, Spirit and Soul of Humanity.

In highest Esteem, Gratitude and Devotion for his inimitable capacity for Justice, Meaning, Empathy, Integrity, Compassion, and the Nobility of his Spirit.

CONTENTS

PREFACE

Yea—for not Zeus, I ween, proclaimed this thing;
Nor Justice, co-mate with the Nether Gods,
Nor she ordained men such unnatural laws!
Nor deemed I that thine edict had such force,
That thou, who art but mortal, could'st o'erride
The unwritten and unanswering laws of Heaven,
Not of today and yesterday are they,
But from everlasting.

SOPHOCLES, Antigone

THE
MYSTERY
OF
CONSCIOUSNESS

A PRESCRIPTION FOR
HUMAN SURVIVAL

CHAPTER I
IN THE BEGINNING

"I am he Who evolves himself under the form of Godhead, I, the evolver of evolutions, evolved myself after many evolutions had come forth from my mouth. There was no Heaven, there was no Earth, ground, animals and reptiles were not, I constructed their form out of the inert mass of watery matter, I found no place there on which I could stand, By the strength which was my will I laid the foundations, I developed myself out of the primal matter which I made, My name is Osiris, the germ of primeval matter, I have wrought my will to its full extent on this earth, I have spread abroad and filled it. I was quite alone. Nothing existed. I lifted up my hand, My hand asked for me as double, And I copulated with my own double. Thus did I pour seed into myself, Thus did I bring forth the gods Shu and

Tefnut. After long periods of time, from being one God, I became three."[1]

Jehovah, Jesus and Allah are now the three sources of Judaism, Christianity and Islam.

The divinity resides in The *Good*, the *True* and the *Beautiful.* Out of this primordial substance, out of the ancient Near East, out of the Mediterranean, there emerged, spontaneously and mysteriously, without apparent extraneous influence as far as recorded history can avow, the *first* manifestation of that *consciousness* in human beings which was to raise the human species above primitive existence.

There was total, if merely implicit, awareness of the universe as though emanating from an inner movement unfolding from its core. Life was not rooted in the isolated individual. It existed in that phase of consciousness that precedes the separateness of the ego and is itself the stuff of consciousness. This aspect of consciousness permitted no differentiation between subject and object. The subject-object content, functioning as the active agent, was the intellect, that is, the conscious mind unsevered from the universal Mind and inherent in it. Thus the birth of consciousness took place.

It was Dante who compared the human being to a horizon constituting the common boundary of two

---

[1]Fragment from an ancient "Hymn to Osiris," God of Creation, found on an Egyptian stele circa XVII Century B.C. by F. Chabas: "Oeuvres Diversés." Vol. 1. Paris 1899.

hemispheres. Of our two essential parts, soul and body, only our body is permanently susceptible to corruption. Our soul is everlastingly susceptible to salvation through grace in spite of the tortures, the twistings, and the evils to which we constantly subject it. For this reason we stand between two worlds, yet possessing the qualities of both, we have something of the nature of corruptible and of incorruptible beings.

And so it comes about that the mystery, the obscurity of consciousness, is revealed through our freedom of choice, our will to choose either the Good or the Evil through our awareness of both. In the sphere of our day to day existence in accepting the principle of our convergence with nature, as an attribute of consciousness, and of grace, as an attribute of our spirit, we achieve the utmost through the infinite unity and productivity with which our lives are then endowed and are consecrated through our freedom and our will to transcend our inherent corruptibility, a mutual interpenetration of the fundamental law of nature and the spiritual quality of grace.

The mystery of consciousness constitutes at the same time a paradox since we employ consciousness in order to define consciousness. Therefore we substitute *awareness* as our guide to the threshold of consciousness. It is then that we experience our hunger and our thirst for righteousness, compassion, empathy. It is then that we yearn to build shelters of meaning for our life. It is then that we see the light piercing the darkness of sorrow, anguish and even loss. It is then we experience the Good. It is then that we find the substance and the spirit of what it means to be human. For we find ourselves in the presence of that creative, inner light and ethical power which does not depend upon an exterior law or activity but rather upon an interior purpose and aspiration of which our outer lives can ultimately be the beatific reflections as an aura.

Thus consciousness answers the fundamental question and aspirations of our nature. It permits through the sacred cherishing of our essence and defines the fullness and abundance of our existence. It does not betray freedom, freedom pervaded by consciousness, and it is ready for every contingency even within the peripheries of the necessary, inevitable occasions in the world.

Consciousness points to the meaning of reality, brings us face to face with its iron unalterability such as death. It is then that our essence or being is the basic and ultimate element constituting reality. Science itself, even neurobiology, cannot solve the mystery of consciousness which cannot, should not, be submitted to empirical investigation or examination. It is like the wind which we cannot see but can only feel. Yet we can observe the leaves trembling in the wind. It is the fruits of consciousness that we can perceive and which can nourish or destroy us.

The bold and perceptive insight of Parmenides leads us to this final truth, that being neither was, nor will be, but eternally is. It is founded in a perpetual present possessing no history since it is inherently unsusceptible of change. It is like the mass of a rounded sphere, equally distant from the center at every point. Such is the true nature for which there is no alternative than either to be (which includes becoming) what we are, or not to be or to become at all. Parmenides' subtle, philosophical poem is something profoundly more than an archaeological probing into the dark obscurity of the year 500 or 450 B.C. It is the immutable truth, the law, so reverenced and so cherished by Plato, and this reality teaches us that this truth cannot be actualized without the ethical conscience whose supreme influence molds, orders, and fructifies all the workings of our spirit and mind.

It is moral consciousness, it is the recognition that a turning with all our heart and soul in the direction of the Good will bestow true well-being not to be measured in terms of practical goods or to be obtained by them, not to be accomplished through self-seeking and self-sufficiency, but to be realized through the ethical, not the theoretical, ideal. "By their fruits shall ye know them." No more precious hope can we cherish than that we may each rise to that height which will reflect in our deeds the moral content for our thoughts.

What has natural science to do with consciousness? In the first place science should recognize its limitations. It cannot, for example, examine through its scientific methodology the noumenon since science is concerned exclusively with the phenomena. Science is inevitably reductionist. Its function is that of fragmentation. Science should become more humble; humility in all subjects is an asset. The program of science is the correlation of cause and effect consisting of a physical state or change. But no examination of consciousness is possible for science. When a scientist looks at a violet, the end organs in his or her retina are being stimulated by a series of waves whose length can be measured; they are about 397 nanometers long; and there is apparently a change precisely to that wave-length in the optic nerve. But our sensation of a violet is not this change in the nerve, and is no more like it than it is like Aladdin's Lamp or the Sphinx; our sensation of the violet is without size or shape or weight or density or movement. It is not empirical. With the faintest and simplest element of consciousness science meets something for which it has no place anywhere in its system.

There is a great difference in the behavior of an individual whether the psyche is functioning mainly consciously or unconsciously. Of course it is only a question of a greater or lesser degree of consciousness, since total consciousness is characterized by the predominance of compulsive instinctive processes, the result of which is either uncontrolled inhibition or a lack of inhibition throughout. The happenings within the psyche are then contradictory and take place in terms of alternating, an a-logical antithesis. In such a case the level of consciousness is essentially that of a dream-state. In contrast to this, a high degree of consciousness is characterized by a heightened awareness, a preponderance of will, a diverted, rational behavior, and an almost total absence of instinctive determinants.

Consciousness is primarily an organ of orientation in a world of exterior and interior experiences. First and foremost, consciousness establishes the experience that something is there. It constitutes the faculty of *sensation*. By this I do not mean any specific sense activity, but rather perception as such.

Another faculty bestows the interpretation of that which is perceived, which I call *thinking*. By means of this function the thing perceived is assimilated, and the transmutation of the object of perception into a psychic content proceeds much further than in perception. Pure sense perception does not provide the data for its own interpretation. There is always the experience of a deeper reality—even a *beyond*.

A third faculty establishes the value of the perceived object which may be called *feeling*. Feeling brings subject and object into such close relationship that the subject must choose between acceptance and rejection.

The fourth faculty of consciousness may be called *intuition* which makes possible the relationship between subject and object which may be love, friendship, mind, and creativity itself.

It is consciousness which postulates existence. Unconsciousness in relation to the one who knows is nonexistence. And knowledge in the revelation of the reality of existence in whose relations the creative element is represented by the ceaseless unsatisfaction and activity of a person as a being who thinks. Creativity lies in effort, in dissatisfaction, in never-ending movement, in the avid curiosity that makes a person a creature of courage, a vigilant explorer wandering over a boundless world impelled toward a goal he does not know and which perhaps does not even exist. Discovery is his destiny and his privilege. Language captures and obediently marks the discoveries. It actualizes them in their symbols. It communicates and transmits them, enabling them to travel through space and through time, making known and manifest to all what until then had been secret and hidden.

CHAPTER II
PERCEPTION

Consciousness is especially important for the understanding of language. Verbal and visual language is universally intelligible and is fundamental alike to all civilizations. A person must know that this is the only path that can lead to higher and deeper degrees of cooperative organization and unity, to higher and deeper degrees of collective conscience, consciousness and individual dignity. Language is the distinctive character of the human being. Even intuition is postulated on the presupposition that consciousness and knowledge must penetrate their object and meld together with it. For as long as there remains any distance between the object itself and the thought of the object, we cannot reach or speak of truth.

But consciousness and knowledge depend finally neither upon identification nor upon reproduction, as empiricism and reductionism demand. Rather they depend upon objectivation and perception—the pristine function of language. For it is then that we may pass from the passive acceptance of quantitative data to a qualitative, fresh, constructive and spontaneous insight into the universe, into nature. Language thus becomes indispensable, not only for the construction of the world of thought but also for the experience of perception, both of which constitute the ultimate nexus of an intelligible communion, spiritual and moral, between all of us as human beings.

With all the stupendous knowledge of details with which science has endowed contemporary humanity, we are not brought one single step closer to the fundamental knowledge of what matter is, nor how matter is related to consciousness. It is merely a name indicating one of those methodological gaps in the world of existence which point in the direction of the world of essence. Once it is admitted and clearly understood that consciousness cannot be mechanically accounted for, not only temporally because of the inadequacy of our information, but as a matter of principle because consciousness is incommensurable with mechanical laws, the impediments to our knowledge of the nature of man may be greatly attenuated.

The positivistic or existentialist philosophies are but a sign of a certain deep want, an inability to find again the sense of Being. This want is now unfulfilled, for these philosophies are still enslaved by irrationalism and seek for the relevance of existence, for ontological ecstasy, in the breaking of reason, in the experience of despair, of nothingness, of anguish, or absurdity. True existentialism is the work of reason. The act, by virtue of which I exist and objects exist, transcends concepts and ideas; it is a mystery for the intellect. But the intellect lives on this mystery. In its most natural activity it is as ordinary, daily and even common as eating or drinking. The act of existing is indeed the very object of every achieved act of the intellect, that is of judgment. It is perceived by that intellectual intuition, immersed in sense perception, which is the common measure of all our assertions, of all this mysterious activity by means of which we declare either I am, or I do, in the face of the world or in the moment of making a decision. Now, when the intellect passes the threshold of philosophy, it does so by becoming *conscious* of this intellectual intuition, freeing its genuine power, and making this consciousness the peculiar weapon of a knowledge whose subject matter is Being itself. I do not here refer to Platonic essences.

"Thou has seen the kettles of consciousness aboiling: consider also the fire." Humanity belongs to one single world community and all the world belongs to all mankind. Personal liberty and social justice now become part of human experiences on earth. We all must finally learn that the meaning of each individual existence rises above the socio-historical process and has a direct kinship with universal truth involving the experience of consciousness in all its moral responsibilities. And in overcoming the dichotomy between individual and social behavior we recognize that the denigration of humanity that has taken place affects each human being in his or her entirety.

This unique and unprecedented universal consciousness distinguishes the human person from any other of the species. Man alone can say, "No." or "Yes." Other species react. Man acts. For *individual* and *social* attributes, though characteristic of the unitary structure of all humanity, are so integral and indivisible that they are but two characteristics of all humanity in its actual existence as conscious members of society. And the events of history in this century especially constituting human designation reveal the violation and dissolution of the inherent interrelationship of man and society in a universal consciousness. The social bonds and identities inhere integrally in human beings in their very humanity. Their relation with the characteristics that distinguish one person from another is so intrinsic and permeative that the individual cannot be either comprehended or fruitfully evaluated unless the societal is included in the examination.

If cultures as well as civilizations are to survive, not in a rhetorical sense but actually, we must cultivate the art and the science of human relationships. For what matters most are not empirical relationships between causes and effects, but the intensity and depth with which human relations are felt. And it is the universal consciousness that nourishes this attribute of life itself.

We must finally accept the necessity of living together and working together, as Kant, Humboldt, Mill, Sidgwick taught, with all peoples of all kinds in the same world at peace, embracing the changelessness in change and the one in the many. The intellectual and moral solidarity of humanity is now a practicable possibility and can be achieved without attempting to obliterate or surrender variations in belief, culture or institutions which bestow and respect pluralism, enlargement of consciousness and vigor.

Democracy when it is more qualitative than quantitative from which the *demos* has not been removed, once the most revolutionary of forces, is now the greatest conservative power on earth, conservative in the deepest and best sense of the term, since it is the only defense and support of the ethical foundations of the world, now almost blotted out in the miasma of doubt, uncertainty, despair, and a thanatological destiny of the human species. Science, once the collaborator of Democracy, has now allocated to itself the position of pontifical authority, forgetting that pure sense perception does not provide the data for its own interpretation. Consciousness reminds us that the experience of reality is more profound, guiding us even to a *Beyond* as we have stated earlier. Those who possess consciousness in all its mystery and *un*explorability constitute a priesthood with all its duties and integrity. Hence the principle of perception reveals its reality.

CHAPTER III
HUMAN CULTURES

Human cultures are no longer the firmly established, eternal and unassailable thing we once supposed them to be. Our science, however sophisticated, our art, however solipsistic, our poetry, however sterile having perished for lack of its pristine nourishment, and our religion, now so sadly denigrated and abandoned, are only the upper layer of a much older stratum that reaches down and penetrates to a great depth, and we must always be prepared for violent concussions which now shake the cultures of the world to their very roots.

Consciousness summons us as a demand of our contemporary societies to do justice to our new responsibilities and to prove ourselves worthy of the gift of awareness and to restore to democracy its pristine revolutionary character by avoiding the act of apostasy. Democracy as an aspect of consciousness in human cultures must not only *be*, it must *do*. For without doing with responsibility and honor it will cease to be. Now on our imminent verge of annihilation, in the chaos which universally prevails, consciousness stirs restlessly in its yearning for truth. But truth itself is not enough. A way to truth must be found. To say that we live for the mere sake of action as action, irrelevant of responsible thought, is to say that reason is bankrupt. Thought and action must be reunited. Therefore an apostrophic plea is made to the conscience of the human species which may be stated in the words: "Milton, thou should'st be living at this hour. 'Humanity'* hath need of thee. It is a fen of stagnant waters."

A passionate and purposeful desire and will must begin to evolve out of the anxiety and confusion of the moral abnegation of our time, the will to concentrate and resist, the will to call a halt, to command a halt, the will to defend the dignity and quality of the essence of the cultures of the world against the corrupting onward march of force, competition, xenophobia, tyranny, and impotent fear. The *ecclesia militans* always precedes the *ecclesia triumphans* and so, if democracy is to triumph, it must be revivified even though it has lost the habit and the attitude of its life-giving authority. A vital, ethical democracy is our plea, a democracy liberated from

---

*I have substituted the word "Humanity" for the original word "England."

self-doubt and vacillation, a democracy cognizant of its own indispensable ends, cognizant of its universal applicability, and of the necessity to foster the growth of an integrated, intrepid, creative human society, thereby curing its disease of decay in all human cultures.

Consciousness bestows upon us the responsibility of nourishing the growth of the spirit and mind, attributes with which we are endowed by nature. Let us not fail. Let us build shelters of meaning, empathy and compassion for the fleeting moment our lives fill, struggling for the ray of light that pierces through the darkness of our time. This is the true meaning of what it means to be human. The forces of good desperately need our support against the forces of that which is worse than evil: *indifference.*

Why our emphasis on consciousness and its universal reality? The answer is to be found in the history of reason itself. Plato in The Republic reminds us of our responsibility to respect and appropriately include consciousness as an aspect of justice as it is depicted in classical Greek texts containing the trinity of the Good, the True, and the Beautiful. "There's a divinity that shapes our ends roughhew them though we will." So Hamlet speaks as does Fred Hoyle in his "Intelligent Universe." Does the Universe possess consciousness? Does the Universe think? Has the Universe a brain? Has the Universe a mind, a cosmic mind? Does the Universe know, is it conscious of what step to take before it takes that step as Fred Hoyle maintains? Do animals possess consciousness? Some cognitive ethologists are convinced that animals have consciousness; are decision-making. We cannot conclude that subtleties of perception in animals, control of behavior by complex stimuli and feats of learning as well as memory may sometimes be interpreted as animal consciousness. Complex behavior in animals does not necessarily imply complex reasoning or processes, nor does complex processing imply consciousness. Animals, as we have stated earlier, react; they do not act. There is a tropistic element in animals; whereas in a human being there is freedom of choice and therefore responsibility.

Even in Democracy, in its valid interpretation, we must restore the hierarchy of facts in relation to a hierarchy of values. Consciousness thus reasserts itself. Then we witness the difference between man and animal.

Let us turn our attention to the principles of thought and their results in human history as well as in our present plight in all human cultures as the result of the denigration of human consciousness and the absence of moral and metaphysical paradigms. Thus we live in a Space Age in science but a Stone Age in morals.

CHAPTER IV
MUTUAL UNINTELLIGIBILITY

During his brief existence on this earth, man alone is free to know, to examine, to criticize, to choose and to create. In this freedom lies his superiority over the resistless forces that pervade his outward life. But man is only man, and only free, when he is considered as a complete being, a totality concerning whom any form of segregation and isolation is artificial, mischievous and destructive; for to subdivide man is to execute him. Nevertheless, the persistent interrelationship of the processes of the human mind has been, for the most part, so ignored, or forgotten, as to create devouring distortions in the understanding of man to the extent that one begins to believe that if there is any faith left in our apparently moribund age, it clings in sad perversion, in isolated responsibility and with implacable tenacity to that ancient tenet: "Blessed is he who

shall not reveal what has been revealed unto him."
For when he does attempt to communicate his knowledge he is for the most part either misinterpreted or
misunderstood.

The mutual unintelligibility among most contemporary thinkers, their apparent inability to communicate the meaning and purpose of their ideas to
those of differing opinions, the paucity of their
knowledge pertaining to the subjects and researches
of others, all this has grown to be as profound as it is
ominous for the future of mankind. And the possibility of clarifying the confusion, which is more than
a semantical issue, and of dissipating the distortions
seems remote. The subdivision, specialization, nay,
atomization increasingly characteristic of religious,
philosophic and scientific ideas, of political and
social movements during the past two centuries, in
spite of the unification of science movements, the
decline and defeat of reason, have proved to be an
almost invincible impediment to an adequate correlation of these very ideas and movements which, in
truth, are in perpetual interplay. The postulates,
categories, dialectical promptings, fecund analogies
or decisive doctrines which first appear in one
eminent province of human thought may, and frequently do, penetrate, through their inevitable diva-
gations, into a diversity of other realms. And to be
aware of only one of them is to misunderstand the
character, kinship, logic and operation of the entire

organism and to obscure and even eclipse the illuminating interrelations.

Human thoughts and knowledge have never before been so abundant, so kaleidoscopic, so vast, and yet, at the same time, never so diffused, so inchoate, so directionless. And human anxiety and restlessness, the dark loneliness and isolation of man amid hostile forces, exist commensurately. There has been little recognition of the importance of a synthesis, a clarification of modern knowledge on the basis of reason, and of the affinity of ideas, a kind of encyclopedic synthesis indispensable if in the future human affairs are to be handled with any hopeful freshness. We seem to have forgotten that all great changes are preceded by a vigorous intellectual reorganization and that nothing new can be attempted in collective human thought and action without a reinterpretation of the fundamental values of mankind. We have succumbed to a conception of nature and mind which has been determined by an incorrect analysis of the phenomenon of life, since it has been torn, isolated, from the whole to which it belongs. Is there no ultimate hope for man to live a well-ordered life, to be able to depend upon the help of his fellow beings, especially upon those who by their ideas direct and interpret the course of his existence? Will not the reality of fear and the equal reality of man's freedom to cope with it permit, in spite of danger, the actualization of human potentiality and the shaping of the world? And is the knowledge which man most requires, namely, the knowledge of himself, to be found only in terms of Delphic ambiguity or in erroneous and predatory understanding?

Out of such considerations as these and out of a concern for the integrity of the intellectual life, its moral and spiritual values, and a hope for the re-establishment of the dignity of man, the plan to bring about a correlation of those contemporary ideas which are not preoccupied with sense data and antiseptic, logical universals, but with the status of values, the bearing of these values on conduct, and the revitalization of reason, had its genesis. Those humanistic men and women, those men and women of reason in the various branches of scholarly inquiry are aware of the principal ailment of mankind—of the disjunction of empirical approach from theory, of methods of observation from speculative doctrine, and of the grave lacunae existent in the study of the nature of humanity. They know that values are eternally present, they persistently question how they may be discovered, they never cease to wonder why they are often confused, and they are anxious to determine in what sense these values are present when they are not recognized. These men and women are devoted to the rehabilitation of reason, reason which has suffered so many wounds during the past three hundred years.

The material necessities of existence and the spiritual values of the contemporary world which coexist in the same complex social totality are functionally dependent upon each other and must be coordinated to assure the stability of civilizations. This work has been undertaken in the conviction that it will be the corporeal manifestation of the spirit of science and culture, of consciousness itself, prevailing in the conduct of human affairs; that it will be a laboratory for the discussion of important contemporary problems with an end to direct the thought and action of mankind; that by gathering in a synthesis, in a crucible, knowledge pertaining to values, knowledge which is Being, not a mere methodological process of knowing, it may at least in part bring back into human society that humanity which has with such systematic contempt and cruelty been eliminated; and that, finally, it may help us to think as men and women of action and to act as men and women of thought with mutual intelligibility. The first step is to recognize that rationalism may not be substituted for reason.

CHAPTER V
THE DECAY
OF THE OLD IDEALS

I look out on earth—lo, all is chaos,
I look at heaven—its light is gone,
I look out on the mountains—they are reeling;
And all the hills are swaying!
I look out—lo, no man is to be seen,
All the birds have flown!
I look out—lo, the sown land lies a desert;
And the towns are all razed by the Lord's rage.
For thus hath the Lord said:
The whole land shall be desolate—
And for this shall the earth mourn
And the heavens above be black—
I have purposed it and will not repent;
Neither will I turn back from it.
At the noise of the horsemen and the archers
The land is all in flight,
Men take refuge within woods and caves,

And climbing upon the rocks.
Every city shall be abandoned,
And not a man dwell therein.
You ruined creature, what will you do!

*　*　*

For the mountains shall depart,
And the hills be removed.
But my kindness shall not depart from thee;
Neither shall the covenant of my peace be removed,
Saith the Lord that has mercy on thee!

But that mercy, that true passion, is the life within us as human beings.

These portentous words from Jeremiah and Isaiah are no longer prophecy and vision. They have become scientific law; they have become the ineluctable truth of mathematics and physics. Man has always known that in the earth, in everything possessing form and structure, predatory forces abound. Man has known also that when the destructive power of even the smallest particles of the material world were governed and restrained, a place was provided on which life could take root and history develop, on which words could be heard, love and beauty experienced, truth discovered, reason esteemed and justice acclaimed.

But what has man done! He has discovered the secret which can liberate the forces hitherto restrained by nature. He has subjected the very foundation of life and thought to his will. And as a result, "gladness has gone from the earth, and pleasure is no more . . . For earth has been polluted by the dwellers on its face . . . breaking the Eternal Covenant." This is the experience of modern man. Is this to be the consummation of history?

Will man pursue his anthropocentric ways, seduced from reason by wily materialism, violent in greed, swollen with ambition, uncontrollable in lust, ingenious in his practice of greater and greater abominations? Or will he finally see through the crumbling of the world those immutable principles and values which alone can bestow upon humanity the intrinsic reality of existence? What will be his choice? How will he exercise his freedom?

The aim of this book is to point out the nascent forces in our civilization. Its purpose is to awaken the consciousness of modern man to the truth that knowledge in order to be effectual can never be made ancillary to merely biological or physical life and experience. It endeavors to evoke the recognition that man constitutes one substance which is both spiritual and material, soul and matter—two coprinciples of the same being, of one and the same reality. It demonstrates the sterility of the positivistic method in evaluating the nature and needs of man and society, a method causing the separation of analysis from synthesis, quantity from quality, phenomenon from noumenon, and fact from meaning and purpose. It considers the basic source of the aberrated existentialism of our time and points to its inevitable growth since its very seminal power lay in our theories of evolution and in our Hegelian emphasis on mere becoming, while repudiating our essence, our being, and thus inevitably leading to an apotheosis of absurdity and despair. It embraces that objectivity of reason in human affairs, in the organization of human communities, and in the establishment of justice which can never be considered mere intellectual achievements but moral and spiritual accomplishments involving the whole of man. And, finally, it demands the recognition that government is a function of the theory of the state, the theory of the state a function of the theory of knowledge, and the theory of knowledge a problem of metaphysics and ethics.

The importunate cry of Oliver Cromwell, echoing down through the ages, may well be repeated here: "My brethren, by the bowels of Christ I beseech you, bethink you that you may be mistaken." It was a plea that man refrain at last from deliberately avoiding existent avenues of knowledge, a plea that is palpably applicable to our pitiful modern society so richly inundated with the potentialities of a deeply moving, fulfilled life, and yet at the same time so desiccated, so impotent to make the leap from potentiality to actuality, to bring finally within the experience of mankind justice, peace, unchallenged liberty and the realization that God's will is at last being done on earth as it is in heaven.

What are the salient symptoms of our decaying ideals? By what signs do we recognize them? They reveal themselves in a boundless absence of any faith in a real order of existence independent of the opinions and desires of the national group; in a resulting scorn and contempt for rational intelligence, except as the contriver of technical instruments; in the abrogation of reason which alone can be a bulwark against a repetition of the errors of nineteenth century individualism and a totalitarian or "communal" conception of society. And, finally, the decadence of much of contemporary civilization is recognized by the irrational repudiation of the human person who uniquely possesses the rational faculty. Freedom itself is therefore stifled, the growth and expansion of the personality aborted, and life itself petrified. For, without freedom, the antinomies of thought and action can never be resolved, and the universe eternally defeats our aspirations and ideals. Unless we can transcend the practical antinomy of being forced by the moral situation both to assert and to deny a moral government of the world, we should be confronted with a universe that could not be moralized. On the assumption that freedom exists, the difficulty is overcome and the universe becomes an order in which the moral law has meaning and the attainment of the goal of our moral striving is guaranteed. In the conclusions to which we are compelled by logic and reason there is nothing to disprove the validity of this postulate of freedom, a postulate which is indispensable to moral action. Indeed, this very postulate is the heuristic force, the guiding ideal, of our metaphysical speculation on which consciousness itself depends.

Freedom, that strength which arises out of inherent human weakness, no longer can mean what the old theologians of Christianity intended it to imply. Liberalism alone is a liability and not an asset. It would perhaps be better if man were able to do only good; but his freedom to do only good, in spite of St. Augustine's affirmation to the contrary, eliminates human responsibility and with it the inner spring of moral life as a thing that flows from human consciousness, conscience, and human will. The whole dramatic sense of life that emanates from freedom disappears and man becomes but an automaton, a passive agent, like a worker in a modern factory who merely repeats automatically the gesture of fitting a screw into its preordained place. Thus man loses faith in man, he is no longer able to find rational justification for the truths for which he struggles, he abandons universal reason and the miasma of a mental and moral poisoning sets in, atrophying life and clouding the spirit. Instead of making use of all the potentialities he holds within him, his creative powers and the life of reason, instead of laboring to make the forces of the physical world the instruments of his freedom, man becomes enslaved, hemmed in by his unconditional devotion to a satanic image, his Self rejected and his soul deontologized.

The rebuke of Zeus to men in the Odyssey might well be the motto for contemporary man: "Lo you now, how vainly mortal men do blame the gods! For of us they say comes evil, whereas they even of themselves, through the blindness of their own hearts, have sorrows beyond that which is ordained."

We present the future by virtue of our comprehension of the past and the present. We recognize the love and humanism indispensable to life on this earth by the wounds which this love and this humanism have received. We have crossed the dangerous zones where the spirit of despair might have seized us, as it has seized other men and women, distorting their vision, and we have arrived where we can point to a specific path for humanity leading to the great firmament, to the freedom of those who recognize the truth and are not reluctant to follow it, the truth that we must learn to live together or perish together, the truth that international morality must be the only basis for human conduct, or there will be no human conduct for there will be no human life; the truth that the ghost of the atom bomb is already shaking its bloody locks in omnivorous greed for another bloody orgy and will yet feast on the bodies of all of us unless we exert our power of reason for our own vindication of men and women, the only power that can save us and convert the deadly potentialities inherent in this instrument of man's ingenuity into its equally creative potentialities for human enrichment; the truth that the moral apathy of present society must give way to a revitalization of the consciousness of humanity.

The ideas in this book re-establish the principle of an all-equalizing justice of Being which can serve as a foundation whereon the sovereignty of intellectual and moral law can be erected; we recognize the depredations following the worship of a subjective self-preservation incompatible with society and man's essential nature; we see that each mind must be something more than a convenient implement in the unrestricted war of each against all; we insist that the state has another end than that of a mere tool in the hands of a temporarily ruling caste for the exploitation of all other men, and we indict that law which exists merely as the expression of the will of the strongest. We denounce those moral ideals interpreted only as a reflection of what society deems expedient, or accepted as a necessary fiction, a formidable facade behind which it can indulge without restraint those egoistic demands of its own existence. We demand a re-evaluation of the moral organism, of all ethical concepts for man and society, and a logic that is not mere formalism and devoid of content but which leads to ontology and the acceptance of the common good not only as a system of advantages and utilities but also as a rectitude of life, an end, good in itself, the true *bonum honestum*.

This book warns us against the chaos that is our inevitable destiny unless we at last exert our unique privilege, the privilege of choice. In us, one may say, lies the power of prophecy for the future. Every work of the mind and spirit, every work of art, of philosophy, of science, is the fulfillment of a prophecy, for it is but the volitional conversion of an idea into an image. So every human being is the fulfillment of a prophecy, for each human being is the realization of some ideal in the mind of mankind.

The history of the evolution of life has revealed the manner in which the intellect, capable of conceiving the ideal, has been formed, formed by an uninterrupted progress in a direction which has ascended through the vertebrate categories up to man. It has revealed in the capacity and faculty of understanding an appendage of the capacity and faculty of acting, an ever-increasingly precise, an ever-increasingly complex and supple adaptation of the consciousness of living beings to the conditions of existence. Thus it should, it seems, inevitably follow that man's intellect is intended to secure the most adequate, the most perfect, adaptation of his body, mind and spirit to his environment, to represent the relations of external things among themselves. But equally important also is a knowledge of man about man. In all the conflicts between the different and multiple schools of thought, this objective remains invariable, unshaken, undisputed. It is the Archimedean point, the fixed and immovable center, of all thought. Knowledge of the Self is the first prerequisite of the realization, of the fulfillment, of the Self.

What, however, during these many years of man's existence on this earth, has actually taken place? How much closer is man to the truth, or truths, about himself? Does he really want to know himself or is he possessed of an unfathomable "Angst," an anguish, in relation to truth? Has he an impulse for knowledge, for truth, even a nostalgia for truth, and yet, at the same time and paradoxically, an anxiety and fear of understanding the truth, a desire to escape from it? At the beginning of Aristotle's *Metaphysics,* one reads: "All men by nature desire to know." It is true that man is impelled by some mysterious, centripetal power to submit to the law of truth in order to be free. Yet the authority of the evidence presented by experience frequently leads one to a conclusion directly antithetical to the Aristotelian position. For man seems to be hemmed in by a pitiful but inevitable dichotomy; on the one hand, he is motivated by the need of freedom and truth and, on the other hand, by the need of flight from freedom and truth.

Let us examine the evidence. The great majority of men are most secure among inanimate objects where their action finds its fulcrum and their industry its tools. The concepts of men have been formulated on the hypothesis of solids, of tangibles. The logic of men has been established on the logic of solids, of tangibles. And the intellect of men has found its hitherto unquestioned sovereignty in the triumph of Euclid and his geometry, wherein has been revealed the kinship of logical thought with unorganized matter and where the mind must merely pursue its own natural movement, after the slightest and lightest possible contact with experience, in order to proceed from achievement to achievement, from discovery to discovery, in the implacable certainty that experience is inherent in it and will invariably vindicate it.

And all this has culminated in the almost incredible discoveries and achievements of science, the perhaps final chapter in the history of mankind, the most significant subject of a philosophy of man and held to be the summit and consummation, the "crowning glory" of all human activities. This much is true: Science is the last step in the intellectual development of man and it may even be regarded as the highest and most characteristic achievement of human culture. It is an achievement deeply refined and one whose multiple potentialities could develop only under the most special conditions. The conception of science in this specific sense did not exist before the Pythagoreans, the Atomists, Plato and Aristotle. And even such an apocalyptic discovery was forgotten and eclipsed in the ensuing centuries, only to be resurrected and rehabilitated during the Renaissance. From that period of the attempted revitalization of human reason to the last demonic acquisition of cosmic, atomic power, the triumph of science remains, alas, complete and uncontested.

Medievalism, too, made one of the greatest contributions to the formation of the scientific movement. That age was impregnated—in an all too alarming fecundity—with the inexpugnable belief that every

detailed occurrence can be correlated with its ante-
cedents in a perfect, definite and conclusive manner,
exemplifying general principles. In fact, the incredible labors of science could not have existed without
this hope. In it lies the motive power, the catalytic
impulse, for research. In it is to be found the instinctive conviction, vividly poised before the imagination, that there is a secret in the universe, a secret to
be unveiled, which can be revealed only through the
methodologies of empirical investigation.

The medieval insistence on the rationality of God,
exemplified as possessing the dynamic energy of
Jehovah and the rationality of the Greek philoso-
phers, found its vindication again and again in the
belief that every detail of existence was supervised
and ordered. There was faith, profound faith. There
was faith in the intelligible rationality of a personal
being, although the trust in the scrutability of nature
was not always logically justified even by medieval
theology. There was faith in the possibility of science, generated antecedently to the development
and exposition of modern scientific theory. And this
faith had its foundation, even though an unconscious foundation, in the theological hypotheses of
medieval thought.

But a general sense of the order in things is not
enough. Something more is essential, It requires but
a brief paragraph to indicate how the habit of exact,
definite thought impregnated the mind of man, especially European man, by the long and uninter-

rupted dominance of scholastic logic and scholastic divinity. The habit abided after the philosophy had been repudiated, which is the nature of habits, the exquisite habit of searching for an exact point and then adhering to it implacably when found. Galileo is indeed the ardent and unquestioned disciple of Aristotle (although profound influences of Plato also permeate his thinking) and owes infinitely more to him than appears in the *Dialogues*.

The progress of science has now reached a turning point. The spiritual revolution is here. The habit of analytical thought has been fatal to the intuitions of integral thinking. Science in its exclusively empirical form, just as thought in its purely logical form, is incapable of presenting the true nature of existence, the meaning and purpose of life, the full explanation of the evolutionary process. Created by life, in definite circumstances, to act on definite things, how can it embrace life, of which it is merely an emanation or an aspect? Deposited by the scientific movement in the course of its labyrinthian way, how can it be applied to science itself, to science in its etymological sense of knowing and being? For man in order to know must be, and in order to be must know.

Or, in the words of *Eckhart*, "people should think less about what they ought to do and more about what they ought to be. If only their being were good, their works would shine forth brightly. Do not imagine that you can ground your salvation upon actions;

it must rest on what you are. The ground upon which good character rests is the very same ground from which man's work derives its value, namely, a mind wholly turned to consciousness. Indeed, if you were so minded, you might tread on a stone and it would be a more pious work than if you, simply for your own profit, were lacking in spiritual consciousness."

Knowledge for science in the Cartesian tradition has been a kind of knowledge that has a certain beginning and varies as it is associated with the things we call realities. But surely this is not all of knowledge. As well contend that the part is equal to the whole, that the effect can re-absorb its cause, or that the pebble deposited on the shore can display the form of the wave that brought it there.

What has been the result of the blind and persistent worship of the ideals of science? Why has an inevitable decay of these ideals set in, metastasizing until the very soul of man is lost, bewildered, without hope? It is because mind has been separated from reason; because man has been confronted with a dualism incompatible with his nature: first, the dualism of the individual and the person, which has dissolved society to the advantage of its parts, overtly anarchistic, resulting in an individualistic materialism which bestowed upon the strong a pontifical freedom to oppress the weak, an individualism which accepted morally and politically Locke's theory that man is a mental substance, on the one hand, and, on the other, Hume's theory that man consists in an infinite association of sense data and sterile, logical universals; second, the dualism of thought and body. We have seen the results of this dualism in the second half of the seventeenth century. Then there was a theoretical contempt for the body and the senses. Nothing was worthy of man but the purity of thought. What did this mean? It meant the triumph and dominance of artificial thought and of false intellectualism; for human intellection can be living and fresh only when it is related to the vigilance of sense perception. The natural roots of man's knowledge were cut. There resulted the inevitable atrophy, therefore, in thought and in culture, a spiritual drought for which the sentimental, nostalgic tears were subsequently to provide a sadly ineffectual consolation.

We must at last concede that not one of the categories of science and of logical thought—utility, multiplicity, mechanical and physical causality—can precisely or exclusively apply to the quality of life: Who is able to say where individuality begins and where it ends? Who can say whether the living being is one or many? Whether it is the cells of the brain that associate themselves into the organism or the organism that dissociates itself into cells? In vain does man force life into a multiplicity of forms, of models. The forms cannot contain life. The models crack and crumble. They are too narrow, too rigid, for what we try to put into them.

Emotional life has been forgotten or has been disregarded. Feeling has been considered nothing more than a confused idea. The existence of love and of will as forming a distinct world, possessing its own laws in the life of the soul, has been relegated or has been radically misunderstood. And our intellectualizing, so sure of itself among things inert, begins to feel ill at ease, uncertain, without direction. It would be difficult to cite a biological discovery due to mere cerebration. And in the final analysis, when experience has revealed how life functions in order to obtain a certain result, we find its way of functioning is exactly the opposite of what we had thought.

Unfortunately, science received its inspiration and its derivation from the least significant aspect of the philosophies of Aristotle's successors. In certain respects, however, this was more fortunate than at first appears but only from a very limited point of view. For it enabled the knowledge of the seventeenth century to be formularized, as far as physics and mathematics were concerned, with a thoroughness and completeness which has its visible and felicitous manifestations today. But it did not hesitate to extend to the whole process and content of life the same methods of explanation which so eminently succeeded in the case of unorganized matter. By doing this, the progress of biology and psychology has been impeded by the uncritical assumption of half-truths. The lantern of science glimmering in the dark, tortuous passages of the life and the spirit of man, has been substituted for the Sun which alone can illumine the world.

The scientific disregard for the spirit and the essence of man's existence has resulted in many distortions, aberrations, and misconceptions, among them being one of the most formidable aspects of modern culture: Freud, with his engrossing, sadistic lyricism which has reduced man to sexuality, isolated individualism and the instinct for death. Life in the so-called unconscious presents itself, in accordance with Freud's conception, as dominated by drives, dominated in such a manner and to such a degree that it becomes the problem of life to obtain release from the inevitable tension these drives produce. This release epitomizes the desideratum of all drives, culminating ineluctably in the ultimate complete release or death; the final dissolution into the inorganic. Thus through an erroneous hypostatization of tension and release Freud, realizing that his concept of a libidinal impulse cannot account for all aspects of man's nature, postulates the inevitability of the death instinct. Life itself thereby becomes, in its very essence, unintelligible and futile. There can be no doubt of the genius of Freud in the realm of investigation and discovery. But his value as a psychologist has been adumbrated by a radical empiricism, a spurious metaphysics, and a too preponderant emphasis upon anxiety.

In no way can one insist that this "ordered" world, which culture represents, is the product of anxiety, the outcome of the impulse to avoid anxiety. And yet Freud conceives of culture merely as a sublimation of repressed desires. What does this imply if not an utter misapprehension of the creative direction of man's nature, of the primal tendency toward actualization! If this tendency were not inherent in man, the existence of the specific patterns of our culture would be completely unintelligible. They become intelligible and meaningful only when they are regarded as expressions of the creative power of man and of the tendency to effectuate a realization of his nature. In addition, for Freud, the unconscious includes all that is inaccessible to voluntary command and the term "preconscious" is employed only for those non-conscious aspects which voluntary command can draw into consciousness. What has been either repudiated or ignored is the life and dynamism of that entire region of the psyche to which consciousness is inevitably linked, the rational aspect of the spirit and the mind. It can certainly not be denied that the free decision of the will, the judgment of the mind, is in itself conscious and indispensable to man's true behavior as man. For Freud there is no free choice, no free will, and even the highest, most objective capacities and functions of the mind are fulfilled in the unconscious. The tragic result of this way of thinking has been a disintegration and dissolution of human personality and unity, of universal reason and objective truth, into a world of anarchistic instincts, sex and dream, animality and matter; in other words, into a ferocious and predatory acceptance of materialism. If science, of which the existential psychological values of Freud are but a few of the many effluences, could be correctly understood, if means were no longer confused with ends, a spiritual purification would ensue for man and a more adequate knowledge of himself, his world, and his relation to the universe.

As a further result of the passionate embrace of scientific empiricism, matters pertaining to social, economic and political life have been abandoned to their own secular law, depriving them of the light of reason. Nothing could be more opposed to the spirit of a social democracy for which the world is striving. Karl Marx did not err when he declared that capitalist society is in a state of anarchy where life is entirely abandoned to the caprice of particular interests and groups. Marx himself is the product of such anarchy, the epitome of modern society, which has failed in its duty to actualize in social, economic and political terms, in concrete, temporal experience, the truths of a social democracy. And by virtue of this failure, society is experiencing a sense of rejection of itself by itself, a profound resentment, a resentment and suspicion against those who failed to corporealize the truth of which they were the bearers and transmitters, a resentment which has created an antagonism against and suspicion of truth itself. Marxism has arisen from a perception of the importance and indispensability of material causality, of the significance of the role played by materialism in the course of nature and history. Such material causality Marx integrated with the dialectical process of history but it became for him unfortunately the source of all activity. The importance he attached to the economic interpretation of existence is indisputably great, but his limitation and his error lay in the principal role and exclusive power he attributed to it. Marx recognized the essential significance of material and physical causation, but he did not recognize its subsidiary, not primary, function in the life of man. He possessed a profound intuition. He saw with deep penetration the conditions of heteronomy and the annihilation of freedom experienced in a capitalist world by means of wage slavery and of subsequent dehumanization. But what he, with so much perspicacity, realized in the existential process of man's life, he failed, because of equal myopia, to understand in the essential, or ontological, process. He failed to see that the masses would one day oppress the masses, that they would be their own greatest oppressors. For if economic slavery and the social insecurity of the proletariat are to be abandoned, if the precariousness of life is to be assuaged, it must be in the name of human personality, human dignity, human reason and human freedom. The potent and compelling exigencies relating to economic life exist only because of man's essential need of transcendent rights and transcendent moral values inherent in natural law, the final source also of economic values. Economic liberty must not be cherished in the name of an anthropocentric collectivity or false communal demands but in the name of the spiritual, intellectual and moral dignity of the human race.

If science, which has made technology possible, is not to degenerate into a quagmire of ad hoc hypotheses, it must develop a criticism of its own foundations, its own premises. It must become philosophical, endowed with an understanding and, more, a willingness to understand man's nature. The knowledge which man most needs is a knowledge of his own nature. At no moment, indeed, in the life of the human race has the pertinency of the Delphic imperative been more tragically apparent. For it has, I believe, at last become evident that the problem of human nature is the gravest and most fundamental of our problems, and that the question which, more than any other question, demands an immediate and satisfactory answer is the question "What is the matter with man?"

It can no longer be said that the absolute is not within the province of science, that we must be content merely with a symbolical image, that the essence of things escapes us, and will always escape us, that we are brought to a stand before the Unknowable. For the human mind, after too much pride, this is nothing but an excess, an exaggeration of humility. It is true that all mental processes fail to grasp reality itself, that they are driven to the use of symbols. Yet all symbolism, it must be remembered, engenders the curse of mediacy and is ultimately destined to obscure what it seeks to reveal. If the intellectual form of the living being has been gradually molded on the reciprocal actions and reactions of certain bodies and their material environment, how can it not reveal something of the very essence of which these bodies are constituted? Action cannot move in the unreal. If man were born only for the purpose of dreaming or speculating, he might in truth remain outside of reality, he might even deform or transform reality, nay, even create reality, as figures of men and animals are created by the imagination out of the passing cloud. But man is intent upon the act to be performed. He is concerned with the reaction that must inevitably follow. The mind of man feels its object so as to receive its mobile impression at every instant. And in this way the mind of man touches something of the absolute, although the contemporary emphasis upon specialization trends to eclipse this fact.

The history of political events and social movements, of economic changes, of religion, of philosophy, of science, of literature and the other arts, of education and even of man's nature, has been investigated by distinct groups of specialists, many of them little acquainted with the subjects and the researches of the others. This specialization was in a certain sense indispensable to the progress of historical knowledge. Yet, paradoxically enough, the consequences proved to be also an ultimate impediment to such progress. For the departmentalization, whether by subjects, periods, nationalities, or languages, of the history of man corresponds, in a real sense, to the actual cleavages among the phenomena themselves. In this way a certain symbolism is obtained which is convenient and even necessary to positive science, but not a direct vision of its object. We must know how the frames of knowledge have been constructed, how we can enlarge and go beyond them. Thus, the mind can be turned homeward. Thus, there can be realized a true coincidence of the human consciousness with the living principle whence it emanates.

Certainly no one questions the indispensability of specialization. But we have come to realize more and more that specialization is not enough. A kind of new scholasticism has emerged as the result of this excessive specialization. We have forgotten that to know only one aspect of man is not to know man at all, and we have also forgotten that the totality of atomic facts is not the world. To be acquainted with only one aspect of man is to understand his nature and the affinities of this nature, its inner logic and psychological operation so inadequately that even that aspect remains opaque and unintelligible. Serious lacunae have resulted in the knowledge of man about himself, serious errors and serious distortions. We must destroy this new scholasticism that has grown with an ever-accelerated velocity around the hypotheses of Descartes even as the old scholasticism grew up around Aristotle.

The remedy for this division, subdivision and superdivision of man can be found only in a close co-operation among men at those points where the various provinces of thought and action overlap; in the establishment of more and better facilities of communication, communication containing substance; in mutual criticism and mutual aid; in the focusing upon what are, in their nature, common problems of all the special knowledges that are pertinent to them. The further remedy lies in the recognition that evil consists in the assertion of some self-interest without regard to the whole, whether the whole be conceived as the immediate community, the total community of mankind, or the total order of the world; the recognition that that form of culture which venerates science so exclusively, so ardently, as a substitute for the religious and moral spirit; which venerates natural causation as a substitute for consciousness and for man's responsibility; which considers the systematic, sterile expediency and prudence of bourgeois man as morally more normative than knowledge and love, leads directly and inevitably to man's doom and destruction.

CHAPTER VI
OUR PRESENT REVOLUTION

The remedy lies in the realization of the nature of contemporary thought, the realization that it is a speculative system-building which finds no reduplication in the life of the thinker, in the life of man himself, and which thus loses touch with Being. It is subjectivism and sophistry. It attempts to find substitutes for truth, such as tautology or systematic consistency. It fails to recognize the distinction between knowledge, algorism and opinion. It neglects with almost Machiavellian intent the directly intuited phenomena of personal existence. It inspires a category of thought which is sophisticated and non-ontological, concerning itself with nonbeing rather than with Being. It results in an abject uselessness of the moral command since it does not touch upon the ontological nexus of man's Being. And its final consummation is a deep and unappeasable melancholy of all life.

Such emptiness can be traced to the incorrect hypothesis proclaiming the relativity of cultural values. Our very positive, anthropocentric and presumable scientific conviction that this world of matter and mind is the only existing universe, this conviction is nothing more than a cultural faith characteristic of our time and our civilization. We must remember that other civilizations lived under the equally unimpeachable and equally sanguine certainty that this is not the only reality. Could this have been a superstition? To declare in opposition to Milton that in his real environment there was not, and could not possibly be, such a thing as evidence of man's spirit not based upon empirical authority would mean presumptuously to render our behavioral environment absolute; to presume to have solved the whole question in advance; and to compel Milton to live in our "scientific" world. It is more than a possibility that a great part of our scientific world belongs to our behavioral, and not to our real, environment.

We must be ready to admit the probability—not yet made manifest by empirical evidence—that every star has a destiny, that its burning matter is so constructed as to make life, consciousness, and history possible. In other words, we cannot deny, on purely materialistic grounds, that the twinkling star, even though it be conceived as a mere machine, is in truth specifically adapted to produce or at least to prepare the ground for producing life, mind and spiritual values. The remote twinkling star may be pregnant with relations which lead to life, mind and history of man—of man as a cosmic entity, as the bearer of values, not merely as an atomized biped without wings or feathers, the collateral descendant of apes—a purely terrestrial, biological accident.

Man in his arid anthropomorphism has conceived the universe as a hierarchic order in which he occupies the highest place. In Stoic philosophy and in Christian theology man was considered to be the end of the historical universe. Both doctrines accepted the debatable truth that there is a general providence ruling over the world and the destiny of man. This concept is one of the basic hypotheses of Stoic and Christian thought. But all this has been called into question by the new cosmology. Man's claim to be the center of the universe has lost its foundations. Man is placed, man finds himself, in an infinite space in which his being seems to be a single and even, who knows, vanishing point. He sees that he is surrounded by mute nature, silent, implacable and impotent to his religious feelings and to his deepest moral and spiritual demands.

Man lacks direction. Contemporary culture is so devoid of unity of purpose, material and method as to be something of a heterogeneous mass of confused entities. Man is uncertain as to where he is going and where he wants to go, and why he is doing what he is doing. Unprincipled industrialism with its boast of liberty, of the autonomy of the individual, has precipitated a condition of society in which victimized men can neither do what they will nor will what they do. Life is overloaded, desiccated, congested, and requires simplification. There is a total absence of organic unity. There is incoherence, planlessness and suffering. There is skepticism and finally cynicism, the predatory offspring of skepticism.

Skepticism has purged the idea of reason of so much of its content that today scarcely anything is left of reason, the only possible common ground for the solution of the problems of mankind. Reason, in destroying the conceptual principles by which it was dominated for a time, soon destroyed itself. At one time reason was the herald of eternal ideas which had only dim shadows in the material world. Then it was thought to find its vindication in the order of natural things and to discover the immutable forms of reality. And now reason is held to be a meaningless symbol, an allegorical figure without a function, and all ideas that transcend the banalities of a given reality are forced to share in the ignominious defeat and disgrace of reason. The synthesis of religion and culture has been obliterated, too. They both must be returned to their one theonomous essence so that the void which was inevitably precipitated by their separation may be filled, filled with a new theonomy. Secular culture has lost an ultimate and compelling *terminus ad quem* because it has repudiated the indeterminate, unconditioned and unconditional character of truth and reason. Unless this

condition can be changed, unless a more valid evaluation of reason can pervade all strata of our society,
it is futile to propagate freedom, the dignity of man,
or even truth.

Society is suffering from the disease of recent
history, the disease that has manifested itself in the
substitution of politics for religion, power for love.
Society has made such impossible demands for an
immediate unmerited Utopia that man's dreams have
turned inevitably into nightmares. Society is beginning
to learn, at last, that there is more human history than
nineteenth century materialism conceived. Society is
becoming suspicious of the shallow optimism that
stemmed from the unenlightened aspect of eighteenth
century Enlightenment, of its ignorance of the dark,
irrational forces in man. Society is beginning to recognize that man must recover what the spirit of religion
has taught him; that there are two ways of knowing:
the exploration of the horizontal, worldly planes and
the contemplation of the vertical or transcendental
order; and that these two ways are mutually indispensable, the one dependent upon the other for its validity
and existence.

An unmistakable thread in recent thought and
action weaving itself persistently through the crisis
of our age and exploding in two world wars within
the memory of most living men is that scientific
pluralism and relativity of intellectual approach
have rendered impotent most of the moral controls
born of religious belief and have thereby given

greater latitude to the bellicosity of men and nations. Both the cultural and the political revolutions of recent history were rejected by religion as the recalcitrant outpourings of a secular autonomy, while the revolutionary movements themselves abrogated religion as the arbitrary manifestation of a transcendent heteronomy. The wild tempest of war broke about us, with all its imperious fury and insatiable hunger feeding on the bodies and souls of mankind. Man was driven, is still driven, his brain mad, his heart wild and wordless. He became inarticulate. Now he is afraid. And somehow underneath it all is the pitiful cry surging from the thwarted dignity of his spirit which demands some kind of redemption that if he must be borne away, let it be by the glacier of life, not by its insidious lava flood.

But man need not be borne away. Reason (not synonymous with theology) can still be his salvation, his redemption, if he will but be realistic and unafraid. Man must realize in the light of contemporary problems that mutual understanding in the field of culture is impossible through means of mere cultural "reconstruction." Cultural disintegration reached such an abyss during the prewar years as to render mere cultural reconstruction an inevitable return to chaos. And cultural chaos is incompatible with mutual cultural understanding. Man is not faced with the reconstruction of those cultural conditions preceding the two world wars. Man is faced with the construction of the prerequisites for a new cultural equilibrium. Man must conquer reason, reason which has suffered and been lost in the wilderness of the past tragic years. Man has wishes to forget that he possesses reason; that very reason which is the only thing that differentiates him from the beast and without which he becomes more bestial than the beast. Man has pretended not to understand any longer the meaning of reason. This has led to the destruction of culture by making him irresponsible for his thought and action. The contemporary contempt for reason has become the tragicomedy of our time. A life of initiative, of creativity, not impeded by ill-conceived and irrelevant planning, drawing its energies from reason in its fullness and richness—this is the first prerequisite for mutual understanding among men and the only way, if it is not yet too late, of preventing another war.

Reason must no longer be confused with efficiency as it had been by political fascism. When the dictators appealed to reason, they wished to imply that they possessed the most guns and tanks and ammunition. They were rational enough to build them; others should be rational enough to yield to them. In reality there is an intimate relationship between reason and efficiency, the causes being inherent in the basic structure of society itself. Only the sequence, however, is important. It is reason compatible with man's potential fulfillment as a being possessing dignity that must dictate the methods efficiency must adopt, and not vice versa. For man can fulfill himself and his natural needs only through social and spiritual channels. Use is a social category and reason pursues it in all the phases of competitive society.

The Revolution is here; and we hope with all the passion of our wills and being that it will not be bloody. There is still a chance that a true social democracy (not an aberration of recent history euphemistically employing this term), which makes its means proportionate to its ends, may prove that there is a democratic solution for the issues of fundamental change which are emergent in society. To prove that this is so would mark an epoch in social thought as important in the imagination of man as the Reformation or the geographical discoveries of the fifteenth or the sixteenth centuries. It would drive forward the boundaries of freedom to an extent we cannot now conceive. And this is all the more urgent since man is clearly at one of the great turning points of history: the necessity for laying the foundations of individual liberty within the fabric of social justice.

Since the industrial revolution, which began approximately two centuries ago and has developed at an ever-accelerated pace, each great war has been more disastrous than its predecessor. But this fact has not prevented mankind from resorting to war for the resolution of differences. With the horrible prospect of utter annihilation presented by the atomic bomb, it is difficult to imagine that the people of the nations on earth can possibly consent to participate in another war. And yet this war seems to be imminent; nay, is imminent; is even inevitable, unless men experience a moral awakening and accept their moral responsibility for themselves and their children.

This war is inevitable unless man can mature quickly enough to win the race between civilization and disaster. Man has become scientifically mature but politically he is still infantile. And the most heinous sin of which man is capable is intellectual and emotional immaturity, the sin of omission. Tremendous tasks remain to be accomplished without loss of time. We must begin systematically to reduce, and ultimately eliminate, all the causes of war. We must revolt against the acceptance of international trade barriers and against the aberrated economic reasoning that leads to the creation of such trade barriers. We must extend the geographical and ideocratic radius of democracy. We must repudiate, by virtue of our moral strength and unity, dictatorships and despotisms wherever they may exist in the world. We must denounce the suppression of information and free discussion. We must not tolerate the feeding of people on a propaganda of lies. We must not prevent people from knowing the facts, else it will be too late. Wherever the press and information and discussion are free, wherever the facts are known and the government is really the choice of a liberated people, then people will want peace and can compel the government to maintain peace. Man faces, by virtue of the release of cosmic power, either the prospect of destruction on a scale which dwarfs the imagination and which quickens the dormant apprehensions and fears of what may happen in another war; or he faces a golden era of such social change and amelioration as would delight the most romantic utopian. Man is finally compelled to prove himself worthy of freedom and responsibility. Man is finally compelled to choose.

The first step to be taken by a social democracy in contrast to its hitherto laissez-faire policy consists in abandoning its complete lack of interest in values. The unifying elements in a democratic system and a progressive evolution of the social implications of democracy must be realized. This means that there is an inherent tendency in the present situation to bring to man's consciousness an awakening and appreciation of the values of a social democracy, of the democratic way of life, and a necessity not to discard this for any promise of a better world. Democracy does not mean a shapeless, inchoate society, a society without a value policy, but one in which spontaneous integration of consensus on different levels continually takes place. Cultural groups, denominational groups, local groups, interest groups, professional groups, age groups, will develop a variety of approaches to valuations, but it is essential to supplement the divergence by a technique of co-ordination and value mediation postulated on the noumenal power of reason and objective truth which can culminate only in a collectively agreed upon and accepted value policy without which no society can survive, let alone fulfill itself.

The conception of history as a permanent class struggle is dead, is just as mythological as the ancient insistence that history is a struggle between ideas. That was a sort of economic Manichaeism declaring history to be a fight between the good and evil principles. Political and economic nationalism also is dead. This form of ethnocentric fetishism has been the feudal baron. Like the feudal baron, it has made laws for its own territories and there was no common, universal Law that transcended all territories and precluded individual tyranny. And therefore, in the absence of law, there was war, which always and inevitably occurs when nonintegrated social units of equal sovereignty coincide with each other on the basis of opposing ideologies and conflicting ends.

Law, as a conception of the restriction of human freedom, also is dead. It is rather the instrument of freedom. Freedom within nations became possible when law reached the boundaries. It became impossible when industrialism wrecked the hope of national self-sufficiency and economic systems could no longer adequately exist except under a worldwide economy. Therefore, the achievement of freedom and the escape from tyranny became possible through the surrender of economic, and hence political, sovereignty. The citizen of an integrated society gains in freedom when a universal Law forbids war. And such a law can never be achieved by mere treaties or conferences. It can be achieved only by a legal order, by a sovereign source of law, emanating from reason; by a democratically controlled government which recognizes and accepts the necessity of sacrificing its political and economic ethnocentric sovereignty while retaining its cultural diversity and pluralism.

Because these questions have remained unresolved, contemporary man has been preoccupied with anxiety and guilt, a condition which contains an implied accusation against society's irrationality. Contemporary man has become neurotic with a sapped will which is the result of a bad conscience and social insecurity. He has become helpless before society's habit of pyramiding one rationalization upon another in the ceaseless, shrewd explanation that gives the effect of actuality to the baseless and the nonexistent. Man's present condition is a societal phenomenon and society must be held responsible for it. This is the meaning of collective guilt. There must be a revolt, a scorn, and a defiance of the social structures which create these insecurities in man and incapacitate his sensitivity and conscience in dealing with these structures. The rights of all men must be defended by an attack against the political and economic, the reactionary cabalas that stifle man's development. As man has grown horizontally in broadening his world view, he has also, because of his feeling of isolation in a mechanistic and power-crazed society, extended himself vertically in his philosophy for better or for worse, reaching down into the wells of dream and myth. This much is clear: in other periods of history the categories of living, thinking and behaving were more strictly drawn and bounded. It was therefore easier to know the "right" way of life; whereas today everything is fluid and ambivalent, the "right" way far from certain in the minds of most men. Compromise is the general rule, compromise between idealism and realism, compromise which must inevitably lead to profound feelings of culpability and result only in moral irresponsibility, spiritual degeneration and intellectual degradation.

The cynicism and pathos of modern man may be traced to the dualism and ambivalence which are the result of a heightened skepticism and a heightened idealism, the result of a struggle between a more firm vision of the ideal, especially of the social ideal, and a growing despair of achieving it. Greater knowledge, by its expansion of conscience, involves the possibility of greater sin. Therefore, a deep sense of sin, of the repudiation of responsibility and culpability, is the salient characteristic of our time. Even love has been repudiated, and sexual promiscuity has taken its place. A scorn of love exists. The sexual freedom prescribed by the corrupt philosophy of a population policy or of mere sterile hedonism does not cure the anxiety of the world of sexual taboos but expresses a mere contempt for love. Love has become the irreconcilable foe of the prevailing rationality, for lovers preserve and protect neither themselves nor the collectivity of humanity. They throw themselves away. They degenerate into a state of instrumentalism. What has been encouraged as healthy sexuality is but an expression of the brutal, fiendish rationalism (not reason) that harries love, and the relationship between man and woman has become one of the saddest commentaries of our time. But all this has now reached an impasse. The progress of rationalism leading to the destruction of man has come to an end. And there now remains the choice between utter annihilation and true freedom.

All society is confronted by a mortal crisis, in all its institutions, organizations and associations. Co-ercion in the naked form of war is supreme. Brute force is the only arbiter. Moral maxims and the norms of natural law are ignored. Instead of being an era of peace and order in international relationships, the present century has turned into the bloodiest, cruelest among the thirty centuries recorded by history. The time is tragic. The proud citizen of the twentieth century finds himself deprived of all his values. His cherished individualism is trampled underfoot. He is an insignificant cog in a gargantuan machine operated without regard to his wishes, his needs, his essential being. His liberties and inalien-able rights are gone. Thousands and millions of once proud citizens, heirs of the Declaration of Rights, are tossed hither and thither, pushed and pulled, more slaves than in the days of slavery. The contractual society of free men, with its contractual economic and free associations, has disappeared. The family is in a state of dissolution, of disintegration. With the frustration of man's most cherished hopes and aspirations, the tragedy of man's life is complete. Man is left aflame with sorrow and lamentation, with misery, grief and despair.

But out of the ashes the phoenix may yet arise. Man must know that justice, institutions of law, the growth of juridical processes and structures, and civic and international friendship which must also be embodied in institutions, all represent a principle of unification by internal, moral power, the only kind of unification that can have any meaning or any permanence. The divergence of the Orient and the Occident, that accident of history, is now recognized for the anachronism that it is. The impoverished reality, the epigonous determinism of the West must be re-evaluated in the light of first principles. For in the final analysis the differentiations of cultures may be compared with the multiplicity of dialects throughout civilization. The essential content of the language of the spirit is the same for all mankind. The only difference is that of the words employed, words expressing the same basic ideals and aspirations, frequently even in the same idioms. Verbal and visual language is universally intelligible and is fundamentally alike to all civilizations of the world. Man must know that this is the only path that can lead to higher and higher degrees of co-operation, organization and unity, to higher and higher degrees of collective conscience and individual dignity. Man must re-evaluate and then accept the truth for himself inherent in these words—for in them lies his only redemption: "I am the Spirit and the Light." This is the meaning of the fulfilled personality. And this requires the communication of knowledge and of love. For it is the spirit in man that transports him, unlike other species of life, beyond the sense of complete independence, complete "individualism," to a sense of personality and communion which unites man with man. Man cannot live in that isolated unity, lacking windows and doors, of the Leibnitzian monad. Each man is a person and by virtue of this fact expresses himself to himself as well as to others. Without this communication man inevitably slips into a preoccupation with death and the solipsistic solitude of the existentialist world. The self-hood of the human person is the tragedy of modern man, as is the progressive, activated rationalism manifesting itself so ubiquitously as the modern substitute for knowledge and reason in the name of which civilization is espoused. This subjectivity of reason which has culminated not in the preservation of the human person but in his disintegration, this prerogative (the offspring of subjectivity) of yielding to a partial inclination, a partial commitment resulting in the starvation of the mind and spirit, must now be transcended by the truth inherent in the objectivity of reason, in the existence of reason as a generative principle not only in the individual mind but in the objective world, in the relationship between man and society, man and man, man and nature. These are forever participating in the creation of one another while remaining solitary throughout. Although they are not one, they are yet inseparable, since there is a boundless manifold of universal potentiality perpetually actualizing itself in a multiplicity of subjects. The objectivity of reason is the only force that can create concepts of knowledge, the greatest good, and the meaning of human destiny, salvation, beauty and the way of actualizing ultimate ends. Such reason must be exhumed from the realm of myth and legend in which it has so irreverently been interred and must be restored to its rightful place with the great philosophical systems of Plato and Aristotle, restored to its hierarchical position of apostolic power in the history of mankind, a position which does not exclude subjective reason from playing its appropriate and logical role, but which recognizes that subjectivity is only a limited aspect of universal reason from which the ultimate values for men and things emanate. This alone can reinstate the dialectic of thought and eros without which experience degenerates into unilaterality and meaninglessness. Man must embrace at least the responsibility for himself and his fellow men that it is "your honor henceforth not whence ye come, but whither ye go."

CHAPTER VII
THE SUPREMACY
OF CONSCIOUSNESS

We have endeavored to point out the one inexpugnable fact of contemporary society, the fact that if civilization is to survive, not in a rhetorical sense but actually, man must cultivate the art and the science of human relationships. For what matters most are not empirical relations between causes and effects, but the intensity and depth with which human relations are felt. Man must finally accept the necessity of living together and working together with all peoples of all kinds in the same world, at peace. With unity of purpose we hope to reveal the fundamental truth in the life of modern man, to point out the changeless in the changing, the one in the many. Intellectual and moral solidarity of humanity is now a practical possibility and can be achieved without attempting to obliterate or surrender variations in belief, culture or institutions which bestow upon mankind its pluralism, richness and vigor. Thus we do not dishonor consciousness.

Human culture is not the firmly established, eternal and unassailable thing we once supposed it to be. Our science, our art, our literature and our religion are only the upper layer of a much older stratum that reaches down and penetrates to a great depth, and we must always be prepared for violent concussions which may shake our cultural world and out social order to their very roots. We have reiterated the demand of our modern society that in order to do justice to our new responsibility, to our consciousness, and to prove ourselves worthy of both, we must restore to democracy its pristine revolutionary character. Democracy cannot merely be; it must do. For without doing, it will cease to be, is in fact on the verge of imminent destruction. The truth itself is not enough. A way to the truth must be found. To say that man lives for the mere sake of action as action, irrelevant of the thought it carries out, would of course be to say that no reasonable purpose is possible. Thought and action must be reunited. Therefore this apostrophic plea is made to the conscience and consciousness of modern man—a plea to re-evaluate the fundamental premises of democracy, to restore the nexus between being and doing, between spirit and matter.

Humanity, true humanity which democracy makes possible, moreover, has combined the individual and the social principles in a manner that is irrefutable and wholly natural. Democracy makes clear that no act of submission can exist, no subjective agreement by which man is able to renounce his condition of being a free agent and enslave himself. For by such an act of repudiation he would abandon that very character which constitutes his essence and nature: he would abandon his very humanity. The value in dignity, which democracy bestows upon the individual being and upon the human soul in its immediate relationship to absolute truth, is not contradicted by the principle of the equality of all men. It is the statute of human rights, this consciousness heritage of the great bourgeois revolution, that both principles, the individualistic and the social, freedom and equality, are combined, interrelated and mutually justify each other. It cannot be denied that all collectivity tends to exaggerate the mechanization, the bureaucratization, the regimentation of man and to submerge the individual and the group in a pragmatic uniformity, even in a conformity, and in mass movements. There is a certain fear for the disappearance of human liberty and individual values in the deep and often unnavigable waters of collectivity. One may say that it is "democracy's fear of itself"—a fear potently conducive to the spiritual distress and moral emasculation from which democracy has suffered. There would be no hope for democracy if it had to choose between anarchy, chaos and the extreme collectivization, or exaggerated socialization that destroys personality and rejects consciousness.

But this is not the meaning of a socialism that recognizes democracy as its native soil, and demands an equalizing justice in the name of freedom. Socialism implies a quickened consciousness to a socially minded way of thought and action. It is the recognition that man is a social being and cannot exist without social forms, without society, which is so inherent in his nature. And society existing within each of its members has claims which express the totality of its vigor. Socialism implies that a purely individualistic personal and spiritual humanity is incomplete and dangerous to human culture, nay, is not even possible. Socialism implies that political, economic and social responsibilities are essential demands of man's existence and moral life, and that these may not be separated from spiritual and cultural activities.

We have uttered a plea to man's conscience as well as to his consciousness to renounce his past compromising ways and to stand forth in an abandoned and morally leaderless world as the strong and unswerving protector of the good and godly in humanity. Such an awakening will mean the spiritual rejuvenation of society and its moral vindication. Conscious, responsible leadership is the only hope against destruction. Blind leadership will be our doom. For "if the blind lead the blind, both will fall into the ditch."

Further, we have tried to point out that there must

be a re-evaluation of the "common man." The *communis homo* referred originally not to the man in the street, to the amorphous, inarticulate, anonymous man, but to the immanent deity, the very divine in every man. What we demand also is something other than a quantitative standard of living. We demand a reinterpretation of democracy which recognizes that an evaluation of equality and justice must be made in accordance with proportionate and analogical truth rather than merely in numerical terms. We demand a form of society in which all work has an inherent dignity and a close relation with the perfection of our personality. We demand a basis for communication, understanding and agreement, for effective co-operation in the application of the commonly recognized spiritual values to the solution of contingent problems of organization and conduct. We demand that our decaying civilization be "renewed in knowledge," as St. Paul declared; not in reference to the facts of science exclusively but in reference to our Self as the only hope of restoring meaning and value to a world of impoverished reality. We demand a "world" in which the concept of vocation is revitalized, not as a mere matter of arbitrary choice, or of passive determination by pecuniary needs, but of occupation to which one is ineluctably summoned by one's own nature and in which each man can develop not only the perfection of his product or profession but his very entelechy itself. Work is made for the man; not man for the work. The primary purpose is to provide simultaneously for the development and the fulfillment of our human potentialities and for the needs of society. In the final analysis, this is the meaning of justice and equality: that every person should do that work for which he is by nature fitted, thereby enriching his own growth and thereby perfecting himself and society. The highest justice is that which distributes to each in accordance with his own nature, permitting of course equal access to all to the sources of economic wealth and spiritual fulfillment; a natural equality, a political justice which mankind requires if anarchy is to be avoided. For when work is divorced from culture in the highest spiritual sense, when the nexus between them is destroyed, nothing but the task remains and leisure and high wages will not compensate for what has been lost by man's spirit, dignity and integrity in hours of unintelligent, meaningless labor to which an exclusively industrial society condemns and relegates the majority of men. This is the answer to the dehumanized industry, misery and prostitution of contemporary man, and the only hope for achieving a morally unified society and the restoration of man to a common humanity.

Long ago Plotinus declared, perhaps anticipating the ultimate, inevitable unity of mankind, that there is nothing strange in the reduction of all selves to the one; although it may be asked how there can be only one, the same in many, entering into all, but never itself divided. The emergence of the new ideals evokes the recognition that there can be no liberation for individual man if there is no liberation for all mankind. Liberation is not for our self, for this specific man, but for that Self which never becomes anyone; that is, only for us when we are no longer our subjective selves, but have verified the dictum "That art thou." In dividing effect from cause we impose the finiteness of our duration upon the eternity of the soul. For there is nothing whatever that I might obtain that I am not already possessed of. Man is what he knows. When this immanent body-dweller is released from the body, from the bonds of materialism, what actually survives? "That art thou." This is what exists if we include in our individualism all that is not-self; for our end is to exchange our own limited manner of being subjective, isolated, abandoned for the universal's unlimited manner of simply being, and thereby identifying ourselves with humanity. And this is perhaps the only meaning of immortality. It exists when we cease to identify our self with the perishable psychophysical self and when we recognize ourselves in all mankind.

The pragmatic ideals and theories with their confusion of ends and means have given way to the ultimate ideals about man and society, ideals which recover at last the truth about man's nature, namely, that the man who knows himself must see himself in everyone and everyone in himself. One may say it is a kind of unified man as everywhere seeing the same consciousness universally hypostatized, the Self established in all beings and all beings in the *Self*. Were it not that whatever we do to others is thus really done to our *Self* which is at the same time their *Self*, there would be no metaphysical basis for any doing to others as we would be done by. The principle is implicit in the rule, and only more explicit elsewhere. This is the spirit of truth immanent in the new civilization, the divine Eros upon which our very life depends, making possible not only the enjoyment of eros but also the fecundity of agape. Ignorance itself is nothing more than the inability or unwillingness to see things as they really are and the consequent attribution of substantiality to what is merely phenomenal; the seeing of *Self* in what is *not-Self*.

> I was the Sin that from Myself rebell'd,
> I the remorse that tow'rd Myself compell'd. . . .
> Pilgrim, Pilgrimage and Road
> Was but Myself toward Myself; and Your
> Arrival but Myself at my own door.

Man has passed through the straits. He knows that he is adapted by his congenital constitution to the apprehension of natural laws which cannot be proved by experience, although experience is in conformity with them. He has passed beyond the Charybdis of false rationalism which attempted to deduce particular existence from misconceived universals and he has left behind him the Scylla of blind positivism and empiricism which denied genuine universals or by dubious induction tried to deduce from them mythically self-sufficient particulars. He begins to demand the universal truth that gives meaning and purpose and moral integrity to his existence. He begins to recognize that the autonomous will is self-legislating and exercises its causality uninfluenced by anything except itself. It is free. Freedom, man begins to learn, is not lawlessness, arbitrariness or caprice but the ability of the will to consent to and accept universal law. And the free will is always the moral will. Insofar as we act reasonably and morally we act as free men, since our reason cannot regard a moral judgment as inspired by anything except itself. Thus deterministic acts must be recognized for what they are: an interference with reason on the part of impulse. This realization of the universal truth of reason can now be restored to us. Everything that we loved in the past has betrayed us. And our last love—the love that makes us acknowledge it, our love for Truth, in spite of a certain reluctance to accept it, let us take care that by virtue of our own blindness we do not in turn betray it. And even if finally because of our blindness Truth is impossible for contemporary man to achieve, then at least let there be truthfulness, for this may be the only honor and the only moral integrity left to our conscience and to consciousness itself.

Today it is not only the abstract principle of the moral and ethical truths of democracy that must be saved as well as re-examined in new forms, made to

live as a noetic force in the life of man, since the
dogma of theology is dead. The increasing demand
for social justice has to be met if we wish to guaran-
tee the efficacy of the new social order. Predatory
attacks on the liberal intelligence are designed to
annihilate the last remnants of consciousness, of
humanism (in which humanitas is still preserved),
and to frustrate all efforts to bring peace and social
stability to the world. If the new society is to last and
if it is to be worthy of the efforts of humanity made
thus far, the new leadership must be blended with
the spiritual truths of the past. Together they can
bring about a revitalization, a rejuvenation of the
valuable elements in tradition, continuing them in
the spirit of creative evolution without abandoning
them to the liberalism that has languished and
grown apathetic, the liberalism of the deontologized
man. Is devolution to be substituted for evolution?

Such an apathetic liberalism misinterpreted the
meaning of tolerance. It mistook neutrality for tolerance. Yet, neither democratic tolerance nor scientific
objectivity means that man should refrain from as-
suming the responsibility for what he believes to be
true, should avoid taking a stand, or should repudiate the advantages of an analysis of the final values
and objectives in life. The meaning of tolerance is
that everyone should be given a just opportunity to
present his case, but not that nobody should passionately and uncompromisingly believe in and be devoted to and be responsible for his cause. This

attitude of apathy and ennui in modern democracy went so far that man ceased to believe, out of mere fairness, or fatigue, in his own objectives. Man no longer believed that moral objectives or adjustments were desirable, that freedom, like love and friendship, must be won again and again, at every moment of man's existence, through nurture and understanding; and that the goals of a social democracy must never be eclipsed. The challenge of the totalitarian systems more than anything else evoked in man the consciousness that socially democratic societies have a set of basic values in common, inherited from classical Greek and Roman antiquity as well as from the Judaeo-Christian tradition, and that they must be stated and agreed upon. Although tolerance epitomized the liberation from dogmatic authority, it nevertheless axiomatically achieved that static attitude of neutrality in relation to the life of the spirit which inevitably substitutes a relativist rationalism for universal, objective truth and reason.

A common fear on man's part of his fellow man, the horizontal fear so characteristic of man's immediate past and present history, a fear which had its prototype in the vertical fear of previous history, the fear of God, of punishment after death, must be dissolved. The ethos and the ethnos must be transcended and must become one universal whole. The essential character of human life, the thing that constitutes its humanness, is the self-discovery of man and the inherent unity of man. This in the final analysis is the meaning of personality, denoting the general character that distinguishes human life from all other forms of life. To recognize that human life is personal is primarily to deny that human life is merely physiological, or that it can be treated as differing from animal life only in degree and not in kind. It is to recognize that the essence of human life is radically different from the essence of organic life, and that the relations that constitute the totality of human life are radically different from those which form a unity of the organic world.

In the Gospel, St. John declares, "This is the condemnation, that light is come into the world, and men loved darkness rather than light, because their deeds were evil." It is here that the unity of thought and action may be revealed. The discovery of self necessarily involves a choice in the sphere of action. And the choice hitherto has been preponderantly evil. Actually, it must be said that it is not so much the atomizations of science during the past two hundred years that have produced the contemporary chaos, the evil, in society but rather the atrophy of morality, ethics and religion. It was not that science was so strong but that morality was so weak. And finally, the secularization of the spirit and of values has resulted in the deepest tragedy of all. Man has almost lost the capacity to love and to be loved, and therefore to know the good. And in order to be restored he must reinstitute the most significant and nonmaterial of human hierarchies: the order of intellectual, moral, and spiritual values and disciplines. To achieve this man must learn that hate is a part of love, the negation of love; and that evil must be abhorred as a negation of the good.

Thus again man is confronted with the necessity of responsibility, of choice. And if this choice involves a refusal to act in terms of the newly discovered truth, then it axiomatically involves a refusal to believe the truth, and this can exist only through the intellectual effort to repudiate the truth. The truth of the wholeness of life must be restored, a wholeness which counteracts the divisive tendencies of the mind. This intuitive organic wholeness expresses itself in the mythopoeic faculty of man and is a defensive reaction of nature against the dissolvent power of the intelligence. Contemporary man must become his own prophet. He must become the prophet and the architect of the new world social democracy. At one period of its history democracy was as restricted in its vision and as narrow in its application as the Hebrew religion at the time of King David. Now the fetters of an established aristocracy, an established church and an established ignorance have been broken. We begin to believe in the potentialities of black men and of men of other cultures as well as of white men. Even as the apostle Paul was driven by the universal implications of the Christian religion, so today we must be driven by the universal implications of a social democracy.

Nevertheless, in order to remain dynamically alive,

in order to be able to state and solve the problems that perpetually arise in human existence, in order to permit the growth and expansion of human personality, Truth must be not only sought but passionately defended when found. For example, the basic discrepancy between social fact and social theory must be recognized, treated and resolved. Man not only must seek freedom from want and from ignorance, but must demand that the new social structure provide freedom for the full realization of human potentialities. In this way the danger of the utter destruction of man by turning him into a destroying force himself need never again be part of his experience. He must at last know that he is implacably and inevitably committed to the thesis that there is a common world which we all must understand, a common human nature which we all share, a common history which we all inherit.

By placing co-operative social action regarding the basic social categories of man's interest at the very apex of the hierarchy of values as the potential synthesizer and builder of the new world order, man will hold the hope of giving to society and to himself, who is the potential artist-philosopher, the key tool by which he may exercise a measure of control over his own destiny. All existing societies are societies imperfectly, since society is a movement toward a goal. And progress consists in the enlargement of the area of rational personality so that it will comprise all people, all religions, all economic stratifications; in other words, all cultural diversities under the aegis of an immutable human nature and common humanity.

But there is another consideration, the consideration of highly wrought emotions and acquisitive designs. Such emotions and designs are a continual threat to the common good that unites individuals in a society. And this is precisely the need for the existence of an international state. Such a state is endowed with the power to curb predatory prerogatives. The abondonment of parochialism, of power worship, of apathetic fear, of a relativism of moral and ethical values, but rather to the embrace of the law of the primacy of the common good over the individual good since the individual personal good is the common, universal good; the embrace of the noumenal power in man by the milking of an inner prescience, this is the fortification of our life, our humanity, our international human society. Human society requires government, but government can claim no end of its own. It exists for man. It is his instrument. It only serves to implement the ends of society. Therefore government must serve as a moral tool.

Thus it follows that if peace is to be assured, moral controls born out of the deepest spiritual and religious needs of man's nature must be enacted. Recognizing the necessity of the universal approach in the affairs of men in our shrunken world, we must demand that the new universal ethical controls are universally applicable and based upon humanistic principles acceptable to all mankind. Scientific universalism has made possible scientific humanism, a system which lacks, however, the messianic power of emotional interest. The universal ethical creed must contain the fervor, almost the ebriety, of a religious pursuit. By enforcing virtue, the state will tend to elevate society to a condition of creative nature. The effect of governmental participation and delegation is to transform a moral law into a natural law—what ought to be into what will be.

The principle underlying the new ideals will be not individualism but humanism which, since the time of Varro and Cicero at least, possessed a nobler and severer meaning in addition to its early vulgar meaning of humane behavior. The principle underlying the new ideals will be the teleological power directing the education of man into his true form, the real and genuine human nature. It will derive its inspiration not from the individual alone but from the ideal, from the synthesis of the subject and the object, the individual and the universal. And this ideal of human character, which it must be the aim of the new civilization to educate each man to achieve is not an empty abstract pattern existing beyond time and space. It is a living, life-giving dynamic force. Above man as an integral aspect of the horde and man as a supposedly independent personality stands man as an ideal, the fulfillment of a prophecy. For when considered merely as an individual, as has been said before, man becomes isolated, desolate in his atomization of the organic unity of his spirit, violated by empirical rationalism. But when considered as a person, metaphysically bound to his individuality from which in truth he cannot be separated, then is he led directly to the absolute, since only in this, his spiritual homeland, can man experience his full sufficiency and transcend the existential world, thereby attenuating its limitations, cruelty and despair. *Such is the responsibility of consciousness.*

What is the ideal man? It is the universally valid model of humanity which all individuals are bound to emulate. It is the recognition that man must be inspired by a philosophy which moves from the problem of the cosmos to the problem of man. And thus the unity of nature will find its counterpart in the unity of the community. Man will find his superior strength in the fact that his mind and spirit will be deeply rooted in the life of the community. We must begin to look at the world with the steady gaze that does not see any part of it as separate and cut off from the rest, but always as an element in a living whole. This sense of the natural and mature structure of life must be intimately connected with the desire to discover and formulate the laws governing reality—the reality of the new universal man. The one law of universal justice and truth must pervade the new civilization, and life and thought must be made to harmonize with this law, the essence of the meaning of consciousness.

The contemporary intellectual interest in the state,

particularly in the international or universal state, has quickened man's consciousness to the fact that responsible, moral men without state are as impossible as a state with-out responsible, moral men. Thus it is that the state, the international or universal state, must compel a choice in man's thought and action, must compel a moral choice, for there is grave danger that if this were not so, there would be no moral choice at all in any realm. The instrumental state is a certain benignant compromise between the ideal society and the actual one. And while there is tension between state and society, there is no necessary or inevitable opposition. They serve to complement each other and to overcome certain divergent tendencies by a superior moral force which binds them together and directs them to a common center.

A tremendous bouleversement has dislodged the concept of independent, autonomous states. A universal, social democracy is the new kinetic power of civilization. The values of individual liberty, of ethnic, cultural autonomy, are recognized and admitted, but the shrinking world, the totalitarianization of war, the acceleration of change, and the rise of a conscious democracy have created universal conviction that when these values epitomize separatism and exclusiveness they can only breed greater and greater evils. In a severely crowded, vertiginously changing, highly powered world, if each part attempts to regulate its own affairs and destiny irrespective of a consideration for the whole, responsive only to its own wishes and its own internal conditions, conflicts will be frequent and ultimate disaster inevitable. The freedom of the individual and the nation must not be permitted to destroy such universal and indispensable values as peace, stability, prosperity, progress and justice experienced on a universal scale.

We are in the midst of a world revolution to which nothing can compare since the Reformation or the febrile forty years which inaugurated the Revolutionary War, the publication of the Wealth of Nations and the Decline and Fall. We are in the vortex of a world maelstrom analogous to the fall of Turgot and the end of any fundamental hope of reform by consent in France, culminating in the categorical surrender of Napoleon at Waterloo. This revolution is crystallizing the manifold potentialities of human society. It is slowly clarifying the principles of international law which, in fact, have been gestating in the womb of history for centuries, and which are awakening man to the necessity of establishing at last an equilibrium between national, cultural autonomy and the unity of world order.

From the heritage of Aristotle, we learn the ontological truth that man's essence consists in being rational, social, free; that acts compatible with man's essential nature are good, and those incompatible are bad. This brings us to the question of natural law (and must be considered in relation to international law) which is inherently reason, a rule of reason for rational beings.

The imperishable words of Cicero found in his *De Legibus* reveal the true meaning of law. "Of all these things respecting which learned men dispute there is none more important than clearly to understand that we are born for justice, and that right is founded not in opinion but in nature. There is indeed a true law, right reason, agreeing with nature and diffused among all, unchanging, everlasting . . ." *Jus naturale* was for Aristotle, Justinian, St. Thomas Aquinas and other moral leaders of history the principles of reason and justice indigenous and intelligible to man, "an ordinance of reason made for the common good," "divine law revealed through natural reason": *participatio legis aeternae in rationali creatura,* and man's necessity to conform to natural law is a command laid upon him by his own nature as a rational being.

Law depends upon morals and morals on consciousness. Finding his intellectual inspiration in the laws of Hamurabi and the Mosaic code, Blackstone in his *Commentaries* declared: "Man, considered as a creature, must necessarily be subject to the laws of nature. This law of nature, being co-eval with mankind, and dictated by consciousness itself, is of course superior in obligation to any other. It is binding all over the globe, in all countries, and at all times; no human laws are of any validity if contrary to this; and such of them as are valid derive all their force, and all their authority, mediately or immediately, from this original." Just as there is in the Universe a physical order governed by physical law, so there is a moral order intelligible to human reason and governed by moral law, e.g., consciousness.

Objective norms of right and wrong can no longer be abandoned in order to pamper the caprice of a dominant group, either national or international, possessing the power to act. Ultimate reason can no longer be abrogated in favor of experience, or history, the pragmatic test, or efficiency. Law must be based on reason, not on arbitrary will. For if law is founded essentially on arbitrary will, no legal provision or decision can ever be unjust, since the lawgiver has the power, i.e., the physical force, to actualize his desired ends. And this presents an inherent, if aberrated, logic whether the lawgiver is a majority, a group or a tyrant. An objective, moral criterion of right and wrong must be embraced, a criterion which evokes the reverence not only of the ruler but of the ruled. There must in addition be a limitation of the power of the national or international state over the community, else law degenerates into a mere arithmetical evaluation of majority or physical force. Finally, man must refresh himself in the wellsprings of his spiritual and moral origins, the ultimate source of objective truth and universal law, or he will perish.

The establishment of such moral and spiritual law will be one of the manifold changes wrought by the moral and spiritual revolution through which contemporary man is passing, changes which first must be actualized by the recognition of a common humanity among peoples since we are all bound together by a more primitive and fundamental unity than any unity of thought and doctrine; we all possess the same human nature, the same primordial tendencies, and the nature we hold in common is a rational nature subject intellectually to the attraction of the same fundamental objects. Secondly, in the economic realm, a choice must be made, a choice indicating whether the immense productive capacity that science has placed at our disposal is to be operated through a system which affords abounding wealth to a few and condemns the overwhelming majority of mankind to live on a standard which denies them adequacy, both in material comfort and in spiritual fulfillment, or whether it is to be operated through a system of nonanarchic production for community consumption. The latter is the obvious choice. Thus there can emerge the gradual freedom of the individual and of society and the realization of their deepest potentialities. Man's social life is not a mere aggregate of incoherent and accidental facts. It is dependent upon judgments which are of the same objective validity as any mathematical proposition. For they are not the result of haphazard empirical observations; they possess the dignity of universal truth. Freedom itself seems to lie in some ratio between our desires and our capacities to satisfy them; between what we can intend and what we can achieve. Freedom depends upon the character of the nexus of relations: personal relations, international relations, man in relation to himself, his work, society, the cosmos. And if this nexus is not a valid one, if it is artificial and predatory, the end can only be one of sterility, frustration and failure. Man must be rooted in truth; he must be needed and wanted; he must participate; he must realize his own indispensability. This is the demand of consciousness.

The old forms have died, died an ignominious death on the battlefield of human indignity and human suffering. What are now being challenged are all the basic hypotheses of that bourgeois civilization which had its genesis at the time of the Reformation. It is no longer possible to superimpose the faith that the mere conflict of private interests, the all too simplified system of the natural liberty of Adam Smith, will produce a systematic, well-integrated commonwealth. We are on the threshold of a new world; a new civilization is in the pangs of birth. We are witnessing the creation of the world. Our decision will determine whether the result will be one of liberation or suffocation. We can no longer demand without challenge that the principle be supported which permits the white man's burden to be tolerated without complaint or revolt by the yellow races and the black. We must concede that during the course of the various stages of historical development the objective requirements of universal reason and natural law should themselves appear to human beings in a way at first shadowy and dim as the twilight. But little by little these requirements appear to lay a command upon man's conscience, they become more perfect in accordance with the development of the moral conscience and the moral will. This apperception has now permitted the full flowering of that objective reality which bestows upon all men the light and efficacy of universal justice and universal equality. These are the new directives. Man must accept this new teleological destiny if he is to master all the potentialities of the new civilization and not be mastered by them. The leaven of equality and justice directs human history toward the ideal of respect for the rights of each human person, and this leaven will continue to work until the end of time in human history in order to eliminate at last every form of servitude.

Scientific cruelty has reached its apex. For good or for evil, science in spite of its many virtues has become the master warmaker, developing new techniques of mass destruction, unlocking the atom to forge out of the energy that holds the earth together the weapon that gives man the final supreme power to tear it apart. Man is at once more powerful than he has ever been before and more helpless in the face of his own power. It would be futile to pretend that the disappearance of historic landmarks and the evidence of the impermanence of all his works will not affect man's relation to life, to the national community, and to the earth itself. It will be long indeed, if ever again, before any political organization will be able to restore the sense of terrestrial security and social equilibrium for mankind. Man emerged from the Second World War torn and humiliated, his soul lost, shaken to the roots, diminished as a human being in his own eyes and filled with a mortal fear.

"Art after art goes out, and all is night,
See skulking Truth to her old cavern fled,
Mountains of casuistry heaped o'er her head!
Religion blushing veils her sacred fires,
And unawares morality expires."

If man is to recover the force of religious truth and the transforming, restoring power of love, if he is to regain moral integration without which life is not life and not even death, he must re-evaluate the fundamental law of human nature and demand that it never be broken again, the law that "he that saveth his life shall lose it," that the will to power is self-frustrating, that the fearless and the upright will inherit the earth. He must know that the truth that "all men are created equal" is a political formulation having its genesis in Judaeo-Christian ethics, that the only community in which problems pertaining to diverse ethnic cultural groups can be solved is a community of humanity in which race is no longer a principle of unity, that the profound social affirmations in the *Emancipation Proclamation* are both political and religious, that the new civilization must concern itself with both religion and democracy, with the individual's relation to the universe as well as to society. An acute consciousness of the tensions between good and evil both within man and in the external world must be maintained, and there must be a recapturing of the living truth in such terms as sin and grace, collective guilt and individual redemption. The profound struggle between reason and impulse in existence, this powerful duality, is not to be overcome by the speculative dialectic of idealism but can be unified only in the vital, dynamic process of creativity, a creativity in which all mankind must and can at last participate, the universal reality of consciousness.

The fate of man depends mainly on the ability to create a universe of discourse—a communal basis— which is paradoxically against the grain of self-assertive tendencies. But one must be aware of this paradox, of the inherent tragedy of human life, without letting that awareness destroy one's courage and one's will. Although Kant, who vitalized the formalization of the new ethics, the attempted reconciliation of individualism and collectivism, was himself unaware of the sociological foundations of his thought, we may say that he arrived at the formalizing concept of the categorical imperative mainly because he recognized that the predetermination of the relevant patterns of action could only result in the limitation of the freedom of the pioneering individual. The demand that man revise his moral and spiritual standards is therefore not so unprecedented as it would seen. What were the Reformation and the Puritan movements if not a penetrating purge of the animistic, magical elements within the Roman Catholic religion in order to achieve a more rational morality? It is a logical and inevitable continuity of this tendency when we begin to demand a collective philosophy which must be functional and meaningful rather than formal, comprehensible rather than arbitrary, and vitalizing rather than apathetic.

In the common-experience philosophy of the future the spirit of community, solidarity and cooperation will be the ideal. Not authoritarianism and the concept of irreconcilable differences, but responsible participation and mutual understanding. And these ideals will differ from the decadent ideals of the past, ideals which were conducive to a laissez-faire, laissez-aller, sauve qui peut philosophy, in the respect that they will substitute for misguided tolerance and apathy a categorical recognition of right and wrong. The new social democracy will differ from the age of Cartesian, atomistic individualism in that it will finally establish genuine powers and possibilities of group life. It will become the meaning of a world-wide Oriental as well as Occidental movement to destroy the frustration that comes from isolation, excessive privacy and sectarianism, and to integrate instead the forces of community life in the service of a social and humanistic ideal. This will be accomplished in spite of the seeming contradiction that the Spirit speaks to the Spirit in the inner silence of individual conscience and that any externalization of the message alters and diminishes its essence.

We are with certainty and celerity moving toward an ear in which the relations of property must be defined in the interest of the masses of people everywhere on earth, the only alternative of which in every organized society being violent conflict. One of the manifold results of World War II has been to attenuate the authority of the men who had been accustomed to exercise it, even to deprive these men of their psychological hold over the masses of people who had previously respected and even feared it. The people of the world are demanding economic and social reorganization, although the custodians of the status quo are anxious, but equally ineffectual, to curb the tides of history.

The ideals of the new civilization will permit, nay, even demand, the re-evaluation of freedom. The revolution embracing these ideals has already begun to exert its compelling force among the masses of most countries, of India, China, Europe and Australia. The bitter experience and the long agony of war have awakened the consciousness of people everywhere to their right to freedom. This freedom, as Heine declared in his deep consciousness, "which has hitherto only manifested itself in man here and there, must pass into the mass itself, into the lowest strata of society and must become people." The change to a conscious value appreciation and acceptance of freedom for all mankind is analogous to a Copernican change on the social plane in man's history, and if permitted its necessary growth and expansion can only result in the amelioration of the sufferings and deprivations of the masses of people on this earth. Thus new forms of individual and collective responsibility will emerge and men will be given at last the opportunity to assume the responsibility for their efforts and will no longer be denied the experience of self-respect derived from the skill invested in these efforts, a denial which has produced the bitter frustration and depression of modern man and precluded the adequate formation of his personality. The educational tradition and the system of values adapted to the needs of a provincial, parochial world must be relegated so that man may be permitted to function on a broad life-fulfilling plane of international unity and co-operation, and thus of individual spiritual worth.

In the early Renaissance, mystical and voluntaristic tendencies prevented the full realization of the human spirit, while Cartesian dualism precipitated the loss of the idea of spirit completely and even of the word "spirit." In Anglo-Saxon culture, spirit became intellect, thus divesting it of its essential meaning and inherent potentialities. Spirit is energy and mind; life and reason. And this recognition must be restored to man's consciousness. Hegel's concept of "Geist" in his early fragments meant life which separates itself from itself and then reunites itself with itself. Later, in his Phenomenology of Spirit, he is driven, alas, to the rationalization of spirit. In Thomas Aquinas, spirit is also intellect, while in Duns Scotus it is will. Anaxagoras was the first to emphasize the supremacy of mind over matter and for him power and mind are synonymous. And finally, and most important, for Plato Logos and Eros are united. It is this synthesis, this unity, which modern man must reconquer. He must return to the dynamic unity of power and mind, universality and personality. This is his only salvation. For the essence of spirit is to think, to love, to be conscious, watchful, transitive. The logos, the Word, must be spoken, must be transmitted, and such utterance cannot be either momentary or endlessly repeated. It must progress, it must vary, completing itself in endless and multiple ways. This is the immortality of spirit; this is its infinity, the infinity of that which can be renewed. And out of spirit, as the fountain source, will ultimately emerge the wisdom and self-knowledge for which the world thirsts, a fountain source at which man may drink in solitude but at which mankind must drink in unity, in society. One cry of moral actuality breaking from the heart of man is his final glory and his final hope.

There is no depth of life without a way to depth, no truth without a way to truth. There is no intellectual and moral meaning in life without an economic and social basis. A social philosophy based upon reality must assert itself against two antagonistic fallacies. It must renounce the pseudo idealism that stems from Rousseau to Lenin, that nourishes man with false hopes and that perverts the emancipation to which he aspires while pretending to achieve it. And it must also renounce the predatory pseudo realism that stems from Machiavelli to Hitler, that distorts man under the terror of violence while apotheosizing the animality that enslaves him. Human life depends upon ideas and co-operative social life, permitting each human person to reach his highest heights; human life depends upon a community of ideas. With correct judgment, correct action will ensue. How profoundly applicable are Pascal's words: *"Travaillons donc a bien penser!"* Tyranny and slavery entered man's existence, hurling him into a vacuum of despair when he failed to accept the responsibility of consciousness, the indispensable moral, economic and political planning for his future. If such responsibility is assumed within the tradition of freedom and with the moral passion to permit man to be free, we shall then realize the new ideal—the creed of the new liberalism. The deep sense of causality, of solidarity, the awareness of values, the spectacle of profound spiritual struggle (and not merely sensitive concern), which the greatest experiences of existence reveal, will be conveyed through the massive, reverberative maturity of the fulfilled and emancipated consciousness.

Peace in the world can endure if the peoples of the world share with one another their common inheritance of art, knowledge and skill and if they communicate back and forth among themselves the new experiences of their lives. Peace in the world can endure if international anarchy can be avoided, if enforceable international law can be established predicated upon the unity, the federation of people, not governments. Peace in the world can endure if human society can finally become as revolutionary in its political and social adaptation as it has been in its scientific adaptation. Woodrow Wilson was the spirit of the League of Nations but one of the most salient influences was Lord Robert Cecil. When the Covenant was finally completed, Hugh Cecil, the brother of Lord Robert, asked, "Will your League work?" And Sir Robert replied, "Think again, Hugh. Does a spade work?" Not an instrument, not a mechanism, but the spirit and will of the people will prove the accuracy or the fallacy of Kant's grim prophecy that the world will be "the graveyard of the human race."

Peace in the world can endure if the propinquity and interrelation of human interests that hold the world together are encouraged; if new areas and techniques of co-operative action, rallying points of unity and centers around which people of different cultures and faiths can combine, are made available. All the products of the mind and spirit: mathematics, medicine, machinery, art, ideas about social progress, the best that every individual or group has produced anywhere in the world, all this must be accessible to the human species.

In his *Reflections on the French Revolution*, Edmund Burke declared:

> Society is indeed a contract. Subordinate contracts, for objects of mere occasional interest, may be dissolved at pleasure; but the state ought not to be considered as nothing better than a partnership agreement in a trade of pepper and coffee, calico or tobacco . . . to be taken up for a little temporary interest, and to be dissolved by the fancy of the parties. It is to be looked on with reverence; because it is not a partnership in things subservient only to the gross animal existence of a temporary and perishable nature. It is a partnership in all science; a partnership in all art; a partnership in every virtue, and in all perfection. As the ends of such a partnership cannot be obtained in many generations, it becomes a partnership not only between those who are living, but between those who are dead, and those who are to be born.

If from the principles contained in these words an extrapolation in international terms can be made of a concrete program of action for a true unity of society, man will not have lived and suffered in vain. In order to achieve this, the term "politics" must be re-evaluated. For Aristotle, for the Greeks, the Romans, and for the people of the Middle Ages, the term "politics" related to institutions, laws, customs,

111

moral and religious ideas which inspired men and influenced their community. The analysis of politics as propounded by Machiavelli, the dissolution of the relationship between morality, ethics and political philosophy, must give way to a new ideal, a new morality, one based upon the right of the human person to have a part, both spiritual and material, in the elementary goods of civilization and the right to demand its effectuation by a responsible world government.

History must not repeat itself. The Enlightenment, that intellectual movement of the eighteenth century, in which the ideals of a liberal democracy for all men had their genesis, although the particular individualism of that period is no longer valid, was in the universality and in the unity of its concepts essentially international. The doctrine of national rights imputed to all men the same rights, and the form of government indispensable to the establishment of these rights had to be the same for all people and all nations. However, more tragic and invidious than the defeat of Napoleon was the defeat of the spirit of internationalism, of universality. An aversion developed among the people of Europe to any universalism, accompanied by a passionate, if insular, preference for their own respective governments whether they were salutary, expressing the will of the people, or not. The world again became parochial. The particular preempted the hierarchical place of the universal.

The doctrine of socialism formulated by Karl Marx in the nineteenth century likewise possessed in its universality and in the logic of its ideas an international rather than a national philosophy. The emancipation of the masses, of the industrial worker particularly, the freedom from exploitation by the "capitalist" class everywhere in the world, was the demand of this doctrine. And these revolutionary international ideas took strong root, precipitating a profound appeal to and a last hope for the economic liberation of mankind from his everlasting slavery. But this socialist solidarity was a hollow thing, posited upon the frail foundations of incomplete abstract principles and conclusions, upon hypotheses which took into account only one aspect of man's nature and needs. And finally, since the devotion to these principles had not been, and could not be, translated into an allegiance to a pattern of conduct, the allegiance of the workers of the world found itself more potent in relation to their respective nationalities than in relation to their international socialist ideals.

And society has witnessed, also, during the past few years, the decline of international communism in Russia, and in China. It is this sentiment of nationalism, of ethnocentrism, as the prime mover and principal political force of our age which has now become an anachronism. But this spirit of nationalism cannot be attenuated one iota unless the people of the world will summon the necessary intelligence and moral responsibility to demand their own common good, the good of the social body as the exclusive aim of society.

Thomas Paine, one hundred fifty years ago, said, "We have it within our power to begin the world over again." The twentieth century, it is true, is the bloodiest in human history, but it still can be retrieved. Man can now produce, if he will, a worldwide flowering of the human spirit, a flowering which society has not known since the twelfth century, a flowering which would be fecundated by the sorrow and tears of these last fatal years. Man can now, with conscience and intelligence, make gigantic strides in social evaluation and control, concentrating the predatory weapons of society within the orbit of a world authority and legislating their powers in order to augment the tranquillity and to enhance the dignity of the human person. Man must now move quickly, for the universal brotherhood to which his philosophy and religion have summoned him has become the condition of his survival.

The human adventure comes to be dignified and serious because it demands communication, and communication is impossible in the fear and isolation of the human being, in the repudiation of universal brotherhood. Our fates are not soliloquies. In the pregnant words of St. Paul, we are "all members of one another." The mystical sense that once declared us all children of God can now find realization in the awareness of our common humanity. As individuals, each of us is one fragment of a species, one aspect of the universe, enjoying a unique position and bound by the laws of historical, ethnic and cosmic forces. Thus we are all subject to the determinism of the material and the physical world. But the mind is not a tabula rasa, "conditioned" by external circumstances. The perceptive organs are themselves creative and it is not the mind but the world that is conditioned. As persons, we possess spirit subsistent in us which is an ever fecund source of liberty and creative unity. Thus the command is laid upon us to understand that organicity and unity of the human personality with its unending demand to be renewed in the organicity and unity of spiritual, moral, economic, political and social life.

A new and great opportunity has been opened to modern society and all future society, an opportunity unprecedented in the history of the world, the opportunity to produce a fundamental change in the vital basis of civilized life without resort to violence. Man, now conscious of his rights, with an immutable faith in freedom and democracy, must demand a world constitutional government to enforce and assure these rights. A great, new energy must begin to influence the thoughts of men and become a powerful impulse of human action, a Platonic idea of the state whose thesis is that the first and principal task of the state, international as well as national, is the maintenance of justice. This must be the very focus of the political philosophy of the new civilization, for justice is the foundation of law and of organized society, and where there is no justice there is no confederation of people. The idea of justice is an end in itself. It exists and subsists by itself; it has an objective, absolute validity. The dignity and justice of man issue from moral thought translated into relevant action. The elevation of man issues from this and not from time and space which he cannot fill. Man must then labor to think morally and act morally. This will secure his freedom, and his responsibility to consciousness.

Man has no homogeneous nature. He is a strange, paradoxical mixture of being and nonbeing. And he must choose which will preponderate. For in the words of Pico della Mirandola: Man is neither earthly nor divine, neither mortal nor immortal, but has the power to form himself into whatever shape he may desire as a free former and sculptor of himself. He can degenerate into the lower things which are brute or can be regenerated by the very sentence of his soul into the higher things which are divine. And it is the latter which alone will inspire a spiritual reconstruction of society, if it is embraced with enthusiasm which is essential to man's creativity, enthusiasm meaning that consciousness is in him who is responsible.

Life itself is changing and fluctuating. Even the belief in the immutability of the atom has been destroyed, causing man to pause and say, in awe of the profound cosmic creativity of his mind, *"Le silence eternel de ces espaces infinis m'effraye."* But the true value of life is sought in an eternal order that admits of no change. It is not in the world of our senses, it is only by the power of our judgment that we can grasp this order. For judgment is the central power in man, the common source of truth and morality.

Let us not be oblivious to the warning that a people preserves its vitality only as long as it engenders a genuine contrast between what has been and what may be, and is attuned to adventures beyond the securities of the past. But even if the germ of decay has already set in, inevitably toward the end of such a historical period when thought and custom have petrified into rigidity and when the elaborate machinery of civilization opposes and represses man's heroic qualities, life stirs again, must stir again, palpitating pitifully but persistently beneath the hard crust.

It is this more than anything else that affords the spirit of man its greatest consolation—the gentle assurance of its own immortality; it is this that gives man the resurrected hope to be found in knowledge and in will and the deep realization that there are no remedies which can take the place of the intellectual and moral conscience or that can be of help to that conscience if it is incapable of being of help to itself. The emergent civilization contains a promise: a promise to restore to man his ethical dignity, a dignity which cannot be lost for it does not depend upon an external revelatory gnosis or upon any dogmatic creed. It depends exclusively upon the moral will, on the worth that man attributes to himself, and on his refusal to live an unlived life, the ultimate source of all destruction. It depends upon the comprehension that infinity is mere vacancy when separated from its embodiment of finite values. The notion of understanding requires some grasp of how the finitude of an entity in question requires infinity for its actualization and also some notion of how infinity requires finitude. For example, Buddhism in emphasizing the sheer infinity of the divine principle robbed its practical influence of energetic, originative value and activity. And every concrete unity of experience must be fecundated by the rediscovery of the generative principles of knowledge, worth, beauty, love, salvation—all requirements of consciousness.

The world of activity is emphasized by the multiplicity of mortal things. It is creative, originative. It anticipates the future, transforms the past, originates the present. But the continuity and transition must never be omitted, for if this is done, mere immediate creation loses its meaning, destroys the existence of value, and the absence of value obliterates any possibility for the exercise of reason. Value demands persistence. In its very essence value is timeless and immortal. It is not rooted in any ephemeral occasion, and the value intrinsic to the universe has an inherent independence of any moment of time; yet it is divested of any authority or meaning when separated from its essential relevance to the immediate world of transient fact.

The primary metaphysical nature of being is the convergence of potentiality and actuality, the interpenetration of spirit and nature. It is the originative source of the qualitative variations and differentiations among all possible forms, and thus of value. Even the contention of natural science asserting the primacy of nature at once establishes the absolute sovereignty of spirit, since it is consciousness that has conceptualized this primacy of nature, thereby rendering all things subservient to the noumenal power of spirit. Yet any attempt to hypostatize the polarity of spirit and nature precipitates man into a dualistic world of absolute spirit manifesting itself in idealism, or some form of mythology, on the one hand; or absolute nature manifesting itself in naturalism, or some form of materialism, on the other. And this postulate of an ultimate duality, this contradiction, is untenable by virtue of the very content of these concepts. Although they are not absolute antinomies, they yet exist in an antinomic world. At the same time they cannot be reduced to each other or to any monistic principle. They are simply intertwined with each other, inseparably related, and every spiritual act implies some form of nature, of matter, and ultimate consciousness.

The function of philosophy is to evoke the recognition of this truth in man's consciousness. In this sense philosophy is like art in that it reflects passion through language, thereby illuminating the sphere of memory and experience, epitomizing through language the inherent crisis in which the permanent merely ostensibly, not actually, is opposed to the transient, being to becoming, and spirit to nature. The longings of the oppressed mind and the "escape from the loneliness of a closed consciousness" are reflected in the universal medium of language which holds indisputable preeminence in the hierarchy of generative principles.

In thus rediscovering a conceptual frame of reference, man will re-experience his capacity for originative value by re-experiencing simultaneously what is universally good through the actualization of his uncreated perfection and through the realization in each being of a plan immanent in its substance. Man will no longer be absorbed with the mere sterile enunciation of abstract principles and doctrines, but his existence will be suffused with the implicit suggestion of the concrete unity and organicity of all experience whereby every abstract principle derives its vitality and life. A new concept of man has been born, a new hope for unity and fulfillment, a hope which can now lead him over the Jordan into the Promised Land, into the calm serenity of the rising sun, and the hope of a new day. Man has met man at Golgotha. Let there not be another Crucifixion! i.e. *the human species.*

In some remote region of our consciousness unity whispers that everything exists at the courtesy of everything else. In other words there can be no separation of subject from object. The unity of nature must be postulated, for if it did not exist, if there were no inherent unity and consistency in nature, there would be no possibility of knowledge.

We are concerned with the unitary structure of all nature. At the beginning, as we see in Hesiod's Theogony and in the *Book of Genesis*, there was a primal unity, a state of fusion in which, later, all elements become separated but then merge again. However, out of the unity there emerges the separation of parts of opposite elements. These opposites intersect, reunite in meteoric phenomena and in individual living things. Yet, in spite of the immense diversity of creation a profound underlying convergence exists in all nature. And the principle of the conservation of energy simply signifies that there is a *something* that remains constant, and we say that the law of conservation is the physical expression of the elements by which nature makes itself known to us.

It is not enough to consider the mutual entanglement of nature and humanity in relation to aesthetic feeling or the perception of beauty. We are summoned to re-examine all aspects of human endeavor which the specialist was taught to believe he could safely leave aside. It is then that we discover the structural kinship between *subject and object*; the indwelling of the one in the other. We see that present and past achievements impinge on human life and envisage what we may yet attain when summoned by an unbending inner necessity to the quest of what is most exalted in us.

The existence of knowledge and its astounding consistency (in spite of occasional, partial, temporary contradictions) prove the unity of knowledge and the unity of nature. Even though the building up of knowledge has been done and continues. Today by people of various races and many cultures inspired by different faiths, speaking different languages, proves that these thinkers have the same needs and aspirations, that they reason in the same way, and, as far as they collaborate with each other, they are united. In as much as all knowledge aims at the same general purpose, all efforts of the mind do converge and harmonize.

The unity of humanity as a species is an underlying reality which no individual differences can obliterate. The unity of nature, the unity of knowledge, and the unity of humanity are but three aspects of a single reality. Each aspect helps to justify the others. That trinity is but the dispersion of a fundamental unity which is beyond our material grasp but within our human hearts and minds.

Human knowledge is of course very imperfect, not only in the past but even now and later, it will always be imperfect but it is indifinitely perfectible. The imperfection of knowledge is explained and to some extent mitigated by its humanity.

Scientific results are always abstractions and they tend to become more and more abstract, hence they lose their humanity. A scientific theory may be as beautiful as the Hagia Sophia, once a mosque but now a museum, in Turkey. Science can be as human as art or religion, its humanity is implicit, it takes a scientifically educated humanist to draw it out, just as it takes an educated historian of art to draw out the humanity of great art. The same is true of music.

Religion exists because human beings are hungry for goodness, for justice, for compassion or mercy; the arts exist because human beings are hungry for beauty. Knowledge exists because human beings are hungry for truth.

Think of a triangular pyramid; the people standing on different places near the base may be very distant from one another but they come nearer as they climb higher. The pyramid symbolizes a new kind of trinity culminating at the pinnacle in unity since it demonstrates that the history of knowledge includes the most glorious, the purest, and most noble achievements of the creative spirit and energy of the mind. The history of humanity's approach to truth is also the history of our approach to peace. There can be no peace anywhere without justice or without truth. These attributes are the joy and pride of the human spirit.

The Mystery and Supremacy of Consciousness is herewith presented as a quality of the human mind, heart, spirit and soul, as a moral imperative. Man has met man at Golgotha. Let there not be another Crucifixion! i.e. *the human species.*

INDEX

ABOUT THE AUTHOR

Dr. Anshen is the author of *The Anatomy of Evil, Biography of an Idea, Morals Equals Manners* and *The Mystery of Conciousness: A Prescription for Human Survival.* She is a Fellow of the Royal Society of Arts of London, a member of the American Philosophical Association, the History of Science Society, the International Philosophical Society, and the Metaphysical Society of America.

The following was written by Professor Ernst Jackh, Associate of Adenaner and Huess, Liberal Readers of German and Universal Culture in 1968:

> Dr. Ruth Nanda Anshen is a world-renowned philosopher. In 1958, she established the Anshen-Columbia University Seminars on the Nature of Man where some of the most imminent scholars gathered including: Albert Einstein (in his lecture), Werner Heisenberg, Robert Oppenheimer, Jacque Maritain, Hanah Arendt, I.I. Rabi, Paul Tillich, Alexander Koyre, Pope John 23rd, Samuel Terien, Cardinal Bea, Radhakrishnan, Ambassador from India, Noam Chomsky, Lord Hugh Thomas of Swinerton, Sir Fred Hoyle, Sir Bernard Lovell, Edith Porada, Sir Muhamad Safrulah Kahn, President of the World

Court, Alfred North Whitehead, Jaroslav Pelikan, Roger Sperry, the great poet, Paul Goodman, Wittgenstein, Hermann Neyl, Hu Shih, Ambassador from China, Joseph Needham, Serge Alexander Kousevitsky, Andre Sakarov, Alexander Saches, Harold Rosenberg, Bertrand Russell, Benedetto Croce, James Conant, Richard Cirurant, Niels Bohr, W.H. Auden, Donald Griffin, Morton Smith, Adolf Lowe, Karl Barth, Jean Piaget, J.B.S. Haldane, Jacques Hadamand, Sir Julian Huxley, Erick Fromm, Tahah Husain, Robert Hutchins, Gershom Scholem.

Dr. Anshen has the unique gift for gathering these leading scholars into a unity of purpose befitting their roles as the custodians of scholarship, knowledge, integrity, justice. First principles of morality as a heritage to the human mind and spirit were the common theme.

Dr. Anshen is the only living philosopher of the profound Olympian Greek and Roman tradition. As a bequest, she leaves for the human mind, spirit and soul what it means to be human.

Dr. Anshen's most recent achievement is the Anshen Transdisciplinary Lectureships in Art, Science and the Philosophy of Culture at the Frick Collection. Dr. Anshen's distinction as a scholar, philosopher and custodian herself of the Good, the True and the Beautiful by which mankind lives and has its being constitutes an immortal image of the human spirit, and should be so revered.

She has lectured in the leading universities of the Middle and Near East, Japan, and Europe as well as this country on the unitary principle of all reality.